AVIATION, AIR CARGO
AND LOGISTICS MANAGEMENT

A Manual for Air Cargo Handlers and Shippers

EMMY ARSONVAL MANIRIHO

ISBN 979-8-88815-606-3

Contents

List of Abbreviations and Acronyms

ACI	:	Air Cargo, Inc
ACL	:	Allowable Cabin Load
AEV	:	Articles of Extraordinary Value
AFCAC	:	African Civil Aviation Commission
AFI	:	Airfreight Institute
AHP	:	Airport Handling Procedure
AKST	:	Alaskan Standard Time
AMF	:	Airport Mail Facility
AMS	:	Air Manifest System
AOG	:	Aircraft on Ground
AOSA	:	IATA Operational Safety Audit
APEC	:	Asia-Pacific Economic Cooperation
ASAs	:	Air Service Agreements
AST	:	Atlantic Standard Time
ATA	:	Air Transport Association of America
ATM	:	Air Traffic Management
ATO	:	Air Traffic Organization
ATPCO	:	Airline Tariff Publishing Company

ATSB	:	Australian Transport Safety Bureau
AU	:	African Union
AVI	:	Live Animals
AWB	:	Air Waybill
BG	:	Baggage Gate
BMA	:	Baggage Make Up Area
BUP	:	Bulk Utilization Program
CAI	:	Customs Affaires Institute
CAMP	:	Cargo Agent Modernization Programme
CASS	:	Cargo Accounts Settlement System
CCA	:	Charges correction advice
CCR	:	Commodity Classification Rates
CFR	:	Code of Federal Regulations
COD	:	Cash on Delivery/Collect on Delivery
COMAT	:	Company-owned Material
CST	:	Central Standard Time
CTM	:	Cargo Transfer Manifest
DACC	:	Delivery against consignee copy
DGR	:	Dangerous Goods Regulations
DHS	:	Department of Home Security
DME	:	Distance measuring equipment

DPR	:	Damage Property Report
EASA	:	European Aviation Safety Agency
EC	:	European Commission
ECA	:	Economic Commission for Africa
ECOSOC	:	United Nations Economic and Social Council
EDI	:	Electronic Data Interchange
EEI	:	Electronic Export Information
ESCWA	:	United Nations Economic and Social Commission for West Asia
EST	:	Eastern Standard Time
ETA	:	Estimated Time of Arrival
ETV	:	Endoscopic third ventriculostomy
EU	:	European Union
FAA	:	Federal Aviation Administration
FAS	:	Free Along Side
FBA	:	Free Baggage Allowance
FIATA	:	International Federation of Freight Forwarders Association
FIDS	:	Flight Information Display System
FOB	:	Free On Board
FOC	:	Freight Out Charge
FOD	:	Foreign Object Debris

FTR	:	Foreign Trade Regulations
GCR	:	General cargo Rate
GMT	:	Greenwich Mean Time
GO	:	General Order
GPS	:	Global Positioning System
GSE	:	Ground Support Equipment
GSF	:	Global Shippers' Forum
HF	:	High frequency
HST	:	Hawaii-Aleutian Standard Time
HUM	:	Human Remains
IATA	:	International Air Transport Association
ICAO	:	International Civil Aviation Organization
ICC	:	International Criminal Court
ICCTA	:	International Council of Chemical Trade Association
IFACP	:	IATA-FIATA Air Cargo Program
IFCC	:	FIATA Consultative Council
IFM	:	Inflight Manager
ILS	:	Instrument Landing System
IROE	:	IATA Rates of Exchange
IRU	:	Indefeasible right of use
ISO	:	International Organization for Standardization

JAA	:	Joint Aviation Authorities
JIT	:	Just in Time
KOT	:	Kipevu oil terminal
LC	:	Letter of Credit
MCO	:	Miscellaneous Charge Order
MST	:	Mountain Standard Time
MTI	:	Multimodal Transport Institute
NAA	:	National Aviation Authority
NAFTA	:	North American Free Trade Agreement
NOTOC	:	Notification to the Captain of the Aircraft
NTSB	:	National Transportation Safety Board
NVD	:	No Value Declared
OAG	:	Official Airline, Guides
OECD	:	Organisation for Economic Co-operation and Development
PIR	:	Property Irregularity Report
POD	:	Proof of Delivery
PPE	:	Personal Protective Equipment
PST	:	Pacific Standard Time
RAMP	:	Region of Aircraft Movement and Parking
RFC	:	Delivered Request For Comments
RFS	:	Road Feeder Service

SARPs	:	Standards And Recommended Practices
SCR	:	Specific Commodity Rates
SEL	:	Special Equipment List
SES	:	Single European Sky
SHA	:	Security Hold Area
SLI	:	Shipper's Letter of Instructions
SOD	:	Stuff on Duty
SOT	:	Shimanzi oil terminal
TACT	:	The Air Cargo Tariff
TACM	:	Transit Air Cargo Manifest
TASA	:	Template Air Services Agreement
TBD	:	time before departure
TC	:	Traffic Conference
TDG	:	Transportation of Dangerous Goods
TOB	:	Total on Board
TSA	:	Transportation Security Administration
ULD	:	Unit Load Device
UNCITRAL	:	United Nations Commission on International Trade Law
UNCTAD	:	United Nations Conference on Trade and Development
UNECE	:	United Nations Economic Commission for Europe

UNESCAP	:	Economic and Social Commission for Asia and the Pacific
UM	:	Unaccompanied Minor
USPO	:	United States Postal Service
UTC	:	Coordinated Universal Time
VAL	:	Precious or valuable cargo
VHF	:	Very high frequency
VOR	:	Omni Directional Radio Range
VUN	:	Vulnerable Cargo
WB	:	World Bank
WCO	:	World Customs Organization
WTO	:	World Trade Organization

List of Figures

List of Tables

Chapter 1

Introduction to Air Cargo

Air transport is one of the world's most important industries. Its development and its technical and service achievements make it one of the greatest contributors to the advancement of modern society. Logistics and air cargo management is generally the detailed organization and implementation of a complex operation. In a general business sense, logistics is the management of the flow of things between the point of origin and the point of consumption in order to meet requirements of customers or corporations.

Therefore, Air cargo professionals need to be at the top of their game. The present manual provides every aspect of air cargo operations to achieve on-time performance of warehouse management, and shipment of consignments to generate revenue for airlines and transport companies.

The manual is designed methodologically to train professionals who can easily handle air cargo operations which are very complex as precision delivery and safety rely on how well air cargo personnel are well trained.

Objectives

The following are the objectives of this training manual on air cargo and logistics:

1. To understand the air cargo and logistics concepts

2. To elaborate the cargo booking and delivery process
3. To provide knowledge on IATA's Cargo Tariff and Rules
4. To inculcate the comprehensive cargo acceptance procedures
5. To understand framework of carriage conditions
6. To use an air waybill as the official contract of carriage
7. To Calculate air transportation charges

1.1 DEFINITIONS OF COMMON TERMINOLOGIES

Agent: A person or organization authorized to act for or on behalf of another person or organisation

Air cargo is any property carried or to be carried in an aircraft. Air cargo comprises air freight, air express and airmail. Cargo can be transported by passenger, cargo aircraft.

Air Waybill: Equivalent to the term air consignment note which means the document made out by or on behalf of the shipper which evidences the contract between the shipper and carrier for carriage of goods over routes of the carrier.

Air Waybill Neutral: A standard Air Waybill (AWB) without identification of issuing carrier in any form.

Baggage Unaccompanied: Baggage when carried as cargo.

Cargo Invoice: Means cargo booked on credit basis for which bills are to be raised on consignor or consignee.

Carriage Domestic: Carriage in which according to the contract of carriage, the place of departure and the place of destination are situated within one country.

Carriage international: Carriage in which, according to the contract of carriage the place of departure and place of destination are situated in more than one country.

Charges correction advice (CCA): Means the document used for the notification of changes to transportation charges or other charges.

Cargo aircraft are dedicated for the job – they carry freight on the main deck and in the belly by means of nose-loading or side loading.

Combi aircraft carries cargo on the main deck behind the passengers' area with side loading and in the belly

Charges, Collect (To pay): Which is equivalent to the term "freight collect" or "Charges Forward", means the charges entered on the air waybill for collection from the consignee.

Minimum Charge: The lowest amount which will be charged for the transportation of a consignment between two points, irrespective of weight or volume, exclusive of special or incidental charges.

Normal charge: The specified general cargo rate without any quantity discount.

Prepaid: Means the charges entered on the air waybill for payment by the consignor.

Pub Charge: A charge, the amount of which is specifically set forth in the carrier rate or tariff.

Quantity: The unit rate which is lower than the normal rate and applies to shipments meeting specific weight requirement.

Cash on Delivery (C.O.D): Means an arrangement between the shipper and the issuing carrier whereby the carrier, upon delivery of the consignment, is to collect from the consignee the amount indicated on the air waybill as payable to the shipper.

Condition of Carriage: Means the general terms and conditions established by a carrier in respect of its carriage.

Condition of Contract: The terms of condition printed on the back of the originals of the Air Waybill.

Consignee: The person or party whose name appears on the air waybill to whom the goods are to be delivered by the carrier.

Consignment (Shipment): Means one or more pieces of goods accepted by the carrier from one shipper at one time and at one address, receipted for in one lot and moving on one air waybill to one consignee at one destination address.

Dangerous Cargo: Means cargo which by its nature or properties may involve risk to an aircraft, passengers, personnel, or property.

DACC (Domestic): Delivery against consignee copy.

Declared value for carriage the value of goods declared to the carrier by the consignor for the purpose of carriage fixing the limit of the carrier's liability for loss or damage to cargo. It is also the basis for applicable valuation charges.

Delivery order: The authorisation of the entitled party to deliver the shipment to a party other than the consignee shows in the air waybill.

Demurrage: A variable fee charged to carriers and/or customer for the use of carrier owned ULD's or warehouse space beyond the free time allowed for Unit load Device (ULD) this is used for international cargo and when a carrier is having and ULD agreement with another carrier or agency.

Diplomatic tag: A sealed envelope or bag moving between a government and its accredited representative abroad, supported by a "Borderau" which has been officially endorsed to indicate that the envelop or bag contains only official correspondence, for which special security measures are required.

Embargo: Means refusal by a carrier, for a limited period, to accept for transportation over any routes or segment thereof, and to, any commodity, and type of class of cargo duly tendered.

ERG code: Emergency response Drill code as found in the ICAO document. The code consists of a combination of letter and numbers, which up results suggested responses to indicates involving the specific dangerous good entry to which the drill code is assigned.

Freight Out Charge (F.O.C) Cargo: Means cargo carried free of charge on behalf of an Organisation or a person other than Carrier

General cargo: Any consignment other than a consignment containing valuable cargo as defined herein and charged for transportation at general cargo rates.

General cargo Rate (GCR): The rate established for cargo in general.

Gross weight: The weight of the shipment including all packing, blocking etc., also including weight of platforms, special bracing etc., if required.

Live Animal: Means all domesticated or undomesticated animals including mammals, birds, reptiles, fish, shellfish, and insects.

Logistics is the "process of planning, implementing, and controlling the efficient, effective flow and storage of goods, services, and related information from point of origin to point of consumption for the purpose of conforming to customer requirements."

"Logistics is defined as the planning, organization, and control of all activities in the material flow, from raw material until final consumption and reverse flows of the manufactured product, with the aim of satisfying the customer's and other interest party's needs and wishes i.e., to provide a good customer service, low cost, low tied-up capital and small environmental consequences" (Jonsson, Mattsson, 2005).

Mail: Means Air Mail when tendered by Army or Civil Postal authorities against mail way bill analogue Voltage (AV7) for domestic or international carriage.

Mail, Diplomatic: Means Government and Diplomatic correspondence being carried to and from Government Departments and consulates.

Minimum charge: The minimum amount which applies for the transportation of the consignment.

Miscellaneous Charge Order (MCO): A document issued by a carrier or its agent, in conjunction with a Passenger Ticket and Baggage check and which may be used only for payment of baggage shipped as cargo.

Net Weight: The weight of the goods, excluding all packing.

Normal charge: The specified general cargo rate without any quantity discount.

Normal General Cargo rate : Means the less than 45 kg rate, or where no under 45 kg of rate exists, the under 100 kg rate.

Off-line Station service: The surface carriage of consignment from or to off-line stations.

Passenger aircraft use the spare volume in the airplane's baggage hold (the "belly") that is not being used for passenger luggage a common practice used by passenger airlines, who additionally transport cargo on scheduled passenger flights. This practice is known as Belly Cargo. Cargo can also be transported in the passenger cabin as hand-carry by an "on-board courier".

Perishable Cargo: Any cargo which may lose its value due to physical or economic rapid deterioration in conditions, such as food stuffs, vegetables, fruits, vaccines serums and newspapers.

Pick up service: The carriage of outbound consignments from the point of pick up to the airport of departure.

Rate, Class: A rate applicable to a specifically designated class of goods. This is generally expressed as percentage of the normal (45 kg, rate) and takes precedence over all other rates.

Re-delivery: Return of shipment to the party who originally delivered it to the carrier

Refund: The repayment to the purchaser of all or a portion of a change for unused carriage.

Rerouting: The route to be followed as altered from that originally specified in the AWB.

Reservation: Equivalent to the term "booking" means allotment in advance of space or weight capacity of goods.

Through Air waybill: An Air Waybill covering the entire transportation from departure to destination of shipment.

Trace: To locate a mishandled shipment.

Transfer: Movement of cargo from one carrier to another against a transfer manifest.

Transferring carrier: This is a participating carrier which transfers the consignment to another carrier at a transfer point.

Unit load Device (ULD): Any type of container or pallet, in which a consignment can be transported, whether or not such container is considered as Aircraft equipment.

Valuable cargo: Means a consignment which contains one or more of the articles as described in these regulations.

Valuation Charge: A charge for carriage of goods based on the value, declared for the carriage of such goods.

Volume charge: A charge for carriage of goods based on their volume.

Vulnerable cargo: Goods for which no value is declared but which obviously required security handling; on shipments which are particularly vulnerable to theft or pilferage.

Warsaw convention: The Convention for the Unification of Certain Rules relating to International Carriage by Air, signed at Warsaw, 12th October, 1929, or that Convention as amended by the Hague Protocol, 1955 whichever may be applicable to carriage.

➤ **Acceptance of cargo**

Major air cargo facilities are now capable of handling millions of tons of goods each year.

Consignments for carriage are accepted:

- ❖ From shipper directly.
- ❖ Through agent, consignment ready for carriage.

❖ From Interline partners.

❖ Shipper's letter of Instruction: Shipper instructions for carriage shall be obtained in writing on "Shipper's letter of Instructions for dispatch of goods", for issuance of Air Waybill Specimen of shipper's letter of instruction for dispatch of goods.

i) **Shipper:** Provides the Cargo Agent with hard copies of the shipping instruction and possibly scanned images or electronic versions of the trade documents, e.g. Invoice, Packing List and where legally feasible the Certificate of Origin,

In some cases the shipper provides the Consignee and the Customs Broker or Agent with electronic version of the trade documents, e.g. Invoice, Packing List and where legally feasible the Certificate of Origin. Customs Broker or Agent and Consignee may also be provided with electronic access to the trade documents. He also provides the Consignee with hard copies of other paper documents legally required in paper format at destination via courier or by sending with the shipment. Moreover, the Shipper submits the Customs export goods declaration to clear the goods for export.

ii) **Cargo Agent:** Creates and submits the Air Waybill as instructed by the Shipper including the shipper's name in the Air Waybill (AWB) message information and arranges the booking. The Cargo Agent places the Air Waybill, Invoice, Packing list and Certificate of Origin the Freight Invoice in the "pouch" that travels with the shipment. He also provides the Shipper with the Air Waybill, which may be a scanned PDF copy or a signed paper copy of the original.

iii) **Carrier:** The carrier or airline receives the shipment with the "pouch" from the Cargo Agent, makes it available at destination airport and notifies the Customs Broker, Agent or Consignee. Airline provides, if need be, a warehouse receipt to the Cargo Agent to confirm the freight weight, volume and number of pieces that he has received.

The carrier lodges the Customs export cargo declaration at origin and the Customs import cargo declaration at destination to clear the cargo providing any additional paper documents if requested. It delivers to destination airport and notifies the Customs Broker, Agent or Consignee.

The airline also provides, if need be, a delivery note to the Consignee at destination to confirm the freight weight, volume and number of pieces that he has delivered.

iv) Consignee: Provides the Customs Broker or Agent with the paper or scanned Invoice, Packing list, and where legally feasible the Certificate of Origin as well as with hard copies of Other Documents via courier, post, and hand prior to reception of the shipment.

The consignee receives arrival notification from the carrier at destination, when no notify party is shown in the air waybill. Therefore, he arranges pick-up and delivery of the shipment.

v) Customs Broker or Agent: The customs Broker receives from the Consignee other paper documents that are legally required in paper format. He receives from the Carrier at destination the arrival notification, as well as the Air Waybill together with the trade documents, e.g. Invoice, Packing List and where legally feasible the Certificate of Origin from the "pouch" by courier.

The agent prepares the Customs import goods declaration prior to the reception of the shipment by the consignee. The customs broker lodges the Customs import goods declaration to clear the shipment providing any additional paper documents if requested. He also undertakes ancillary services as instructed by the Consignee, such as pickup and delivery of the shipment.

> **E-AWB: e-Air Waybill**

E-AWB removes the requirement for a paper Air Waybill, significantly simplifying the air freight supply chain process, with the e-AWB, there is no longer a need to print, handle or archive the paper AWB.

> **E-AWB Benefits**

E-Air Waybill has the following benefits:

a. Improving productivity by eliminating manual tasks and streamlining processes
b. Reducing processing costs due to the removal of paper Air Waybill (AWB) and the elimination of the requirements to file paper AWB.
c. Improving customer service by speeding up cargo processing
d. Increasing quality of information thanks to electronic data that are used from the very beginning to the very end of the air cargo supply chain.

Checking of cargo at destination station is done as the following:

i) Check that the details shown on packages confirm to details on the Air Waybill.
ii) Check weight of consignment.
iii) Check dimensions/volume.
iv) Check correctness of rates/charges applied.
v) Make entry of each consignment note in the Incoming Cargo Register.

vi) When cargo is received in damage or loose condition record weight both on the consignment Note and in the Incoming Cargo Register. Discrepancy if any must be reported to the Station of origin or en-route station and Regional Commercial Managers.

vii) Transit and 'Airport Delivery' consignments should be kept at Airport.

➢ WAREHOUSING

Warehouses are usually large plain buildings used for commercial purposes for storage of goods. Warehouses are commonly used by exporters, importers, wholesalers, manufacturers etc. Warehouses are usually equipped with loading docks to load and unload trucks and they have cranes and forklifts for moving goods and are placed on International standard organization (ISO) standard pallets loaded into pallet racks.

On-Airport Cargo Warehousing

   i) Air Cargo Unloading and Break Down
  ii) Air Cargo Build up and Loading
 iii) Import and Export Document Processing
  iv) US Customs Border Patrol Air Manifest System (AMS)
   v) Dangerous Goods Acceptance
  vi) Company Material Clearance
 vii) TSA Approved Security Screening Services
viii) Tracking and Tracing
  ix) Container Freight Station Operations
   x) Unit load Device (ULD) Inventory and Control
  xi) Warehouse Delivery and Receipt
 xii) Warehouse Product Inventory

xiii) *United States Postal Service* (USPO) Mail Scanning and Processing

xiv) *Endoscopic third ventriculostomy* (ETV) Systems Operation

xv) Refrigeration Facility Operation

xvi) Valuable and Vulnerable Cargo Handling.

At the most basic level, warehousing is the goods stored in a warehouse. There are many different storage systems that may be used for storing the goods in a warehouse including carousels, mezzanine, pallet racking, and vertical lift modules.

Warehousing happens on different levels. Some warehousing is set up for the direct loading and unloading of cargo at seaports, airports, or railways. These are usually warehouses operated by the port or rail authorities for organizing and storing cargo temporarily for release to shippers after customs and other processing has been completed.

1.2 AIR TRANSPORT REGULATORY BODIES

1.2.1 International Air Transport Association (IATA)

The International Air Transport Association is the trade association for the world's airlines. It represents some 243 airlines or more than 80% of total air traffic. IATA is formed in 19th April 1945 at the Havana of Cuba. IATA supports airline activity and helps formulate industry policy and standards. It is headquartered in Montreal, Canada with Executive Offices in Geneva, Switzerland. IATA is effectively a powerful lobbying body for international air carriers, while ICAO is an inter-governmental organization which deals with regulatory aspects of national civil aviation oversight. ICAO makes recommendations and sets standards although it has no enforcement powers which are generally followed by national civil aviation authorities.

The chronological events to the creation of IATA:

1919 The world's First International scheduled services started.

It has got 57 members from 31 countries in 1945

Today 243 Member Airlines from 126 nations in every part of the world.

IATA MISSION

- *To Represent, Lead and serve the Airline Industry*

IATA duties and responsibilities

- ❖ All the Airline Rules and regulations are defined by IATA.
- ❖ To provide safe, reliable and secure transportation to the Passengers
- ❖ Price setting
- ❖ Price setting body for international airfares
- ❖ 1978 US deregulated the domestic market or open sky Policy
- ❖ IATA assigns a 3 – letter IATA-Airport code. Eg: KGL,DXB,LON
- ❖ 2 letter Airline designators. For example, AI, BA, KU
- ❖ IATA assigns delay codes for Airlines
- ❖ IATA administrates worldwide BSP (billing and settlement plan)
- ❖ IATA handles Cargo Accounts Settlement Systems
- ❖ IATA regulates the shipping of Dangerous Goods by Air
- ❖ IATA publishes the Dangerous Goods (DGR) Manual every year
- ❖ IATA Publishes the standards for use in the Airline Industry
- ❖ Bar code boarding cards introduced by IATA
- ❖ IATA Rates of Exchange (IROE) published four times in a year

- ❖ NUC is used for construction of international fares
- ❖ IATA Operational safety Audit (IOSA) was launched by IATA with the aim to serve as a standard and worldwide recognized certification of airlines operational management.

Moreover, as per the Articles of Association of IATA, *the main objectives are:*

i) To promote safe, regular and economical air transport for the benefit of the people of the world, to foster air commerce and, to study the problems connected therewith;

ii) To provide means for collaboration among the air transport enterprises engaged directly or indirectly in international air transport services;

iii) To cooperate with the International Civil Aviation Organization and other international organizations.

iv) To provide a common platform for travel agencies/tour operators

v) To promote and develop international tourism.

THE FUNCTION OF IATA:

IATA assigns three-letter & two-letter codes to airport & airlines, respectively, which are commonly used worldwide.

Travel Agent accreditation is available for travel professionals. Full accreditation allows agents to sell tickets on behalf of all IATA member airlines. Cargo Agent accreditation is a similar program. IATA/IATAN (International Association of Travel Agents Network) ID card is globally recognized industry credential for travel professionals.

IATA also runs the Billing and Settlement Plan, which is a $300 billion-plus financial system that looks after airline money.

And it provides a number of business intelligence publications and services.

Simplifying the Business was launched in 2004. This initiative has introduced a number of crucial concepts to passenger travel, including the electronic ticket and the bar coded boarding pass. Many other innovations are being established as part of the Fast Travel initiative, including a range of self-service baggage options.

IATA regulates the shipping of dangerous goods and publishes the IATA Dangerous Goods Regulations manual (DGR).

In 2003, the IATA Operational Safety Audit (AOSA) was launched with the aim to serve as a standard and worldwide recognized certificate of airlines' operational management.

1.2.2 International Civil Aviation Organization (ICAO)

A specialized agency of the United Nations, the International Civil Aviation Organization sets the standards and regulations that have helped the global air transport system evolve into a critical driver of social and economic prosperity for communities and businesses all around the world. It serves 191 Member States and acts a focal point for the entire global aviation community. ICAO offers its employees an attractive compensation and benefits package with competitive pay and excellent benefits, in line with its sister organizations of the United Nations Common System. A wide range of professional and administrative opportunities await job seekers from virtually every demographic and skill level, as well as a dynamic community of international colleagues. With the global air transport network poised to double in size by 2030, this sector provides the challenge and opportunity to those who are looking for as they plan their next career move. Adopt best practices and regulations for international air navigation and transport.

The International Civil Aviation Organization (ICAO) creates regulations for aviation safety, security, efficiency and regularity and environmental protection. The organization also regulates operating practices and procedures covering the technical field of aviation. *This collection ensures smooth air transportation and border crossing procedures:*

- Ensure fair opportunity to operate international airlines
- Promote flight safety
- Minimize expenses and penalties

In 1944, 32 countries in US signed an agreement to form IACO as a means to secure international co-operation for highest possible degree of uniformity in regulations and standards, procedures and organization regarding civil aviation matters.

Also they signed an agreement on International Service transit Agreement and international Air Transport Agreement. The Chicago Convention laid a foundation for a common set of rules and regulations regarding air navigation safety and paved the way for a common air navigation system throughout the world.

a. The main aim of ICAO

The aim of International Civil Aviation Organization is the following:

i) Insuring the safe orderly growth of international civil aviation throughout the world

ii) Encouraging the arts of aircraft design and operation for peaceful purpose.

iii) Encouraging the development of airways, airports and air navigational facilities for international civil aviation organization.

iv) Meeting the needs of the people of the world for safe, regular, efficient and economical air transportation.

v) Preventing economical waste caused due to unreasonable competition

vi) Ensuring that the rights of the contracting states are fully respected and that every contracting state has fair opportunity to operate international airlines.

vii) Avoiding discrimination between contracting states.

viii) Promoting safety of flight in international air navigation.

ix) Promoting development of international civil aeronautics.

x) Standardizing international practices in aviation,

xi) Establishing international standards, recommended Practices and Procedures covering the technical field of aviation.

xii) Licensing of Personnel

xiii) Establishing Rules of the Air

xiv) Aeronautical meteorology

xv) Aeronautical charts, Units of measurement

xvi) Operation of aircrafts

xvii) Nationality and registration marks.

xviii) Airworthiness,

xix) Aeronautical telecommunications

xx) Air traffic services

xxi) Aircraft noise and engine emissions

xxii) Search and rescue operations

xxiii) Aircraft accident investigation, aerodromes

xxiv) Aeronautical information services

xxv) Security and the safe transportation of Dangerous goods.

xxvi) Communication navigational surveillance.

ICAO recent achievement is the development of satellite-based system concept to meet the future communications, navigation and surveillance.

b. Activities of ICAO

Regional Planning

ICAO recognizes nine geographical regions for planning the provision of air navigation facilities and services required on the ground by the aircraft flying in these regions.

Facilitation

ICAO has tried to persuade its contracting states to reduce red tape and international standards on facilitation by providing adequate terminal building for passengers, baggage and air cargo with related facilities and services.

Economics

ICAO requires international services to be established on the basis of equality of opportunity and operated soundly and economically to assist states in planning their air transport, ICAO publishes world aviation statistical data, produces manuals for the guidance of the states such as statistics of air traffic forecasting, air navigational facility tariffs and economic regulation of air transport and airfares and rates.

c. Technical and Co-Operation for Development

ICAO pays special attention to promoting civil aviation in developing countries with aerodromes, air traffic control towers, communication and meteorological services.

In response to alarming incidents in recent years of acts of unlawful interference against aircraft and airports, ICAO provides assistance to states in order to improve their aviation security facilities and procedures.

d. Law

International recognition of property rights in aircrafts, damage done by the aircrafts to third party on the surface, liability of the air carriers to its passengers, crimes committed on board the air craft, the marking of plastic explosives for detection and unlawful interference with civil aviation.

e. ICAO's strategic planning

Globalization and trans-nationalisation of markets and operations

Emergence of regional and sub-regional trading and regulatory blocks

Commercialization of government service providers

Liberalization of Economic regulation

Potential evasion of safety regulation

Blurring of sectorial boundaries and responsibilities of,related authorities.

f. ICAO Annexes.

There are normally two Acts which govern civil aviation industry under ICAO namely:

i) **Aircraft Act, 1934:** this Act as of 19th August 1934 makes better provision for the control of the manufacture, possession, use operation, sale, import and export of aircraft

ii) **The Aircraft rules, 1937**

Apart from those two acts, there are also important international conventions to regulate civil air transportation as below:

i) Chicago Convention: The Convention on International Civil Aviation, also known as the Chicago Convention, established the International Civil Aviation Organization (ICAO), a specialized agency of the United Nations charged with coordinating and regulating international air travel. The Convention establishes rules of airspace, aircraft registration and safety, and details the rights of the signatories in relation to air travel. The Convention also exempts commercial air fuels from tax.

The document was signed on December 7, 1944 in Chicago, U.S., by 52 signatory states. It received the requisite 26th ratification on March 5, 1947 and went into effect on April 4, 1947, the same date that ICAO came into being. In October of the same year, ICAO became a specialized agency of the United Nations Economic and Social Council (ECOSOC). The Convention has since been revised eight times in 1959, 1963, 1969, 1975, 1980, 1997, 2000 and 2006. As of 2013, the Chicago Convention has 191 state parties, which includes all member states of the United Nations except Dominica, Liechtenstein, and Tuvalu plus the Cook Islands

ii) The Warsaw Convention: The Convention for the Unification of certain rules relating to international carriage by air, commonly known as the Warsaw Convention, is an international convention which regulates liability for international carriage of persons, luggage, or goods performed by aircraft for reward.

Originally signed in 1929 in Warsaw hence the name, it was amended in 1955 at The Hague, Netherlands, and in 1971 in Guatemala City, Guatemala. United States courts have held that, at least for some purposes, the Warsaw Convention is a different instrument from the Warsaw Convention as amended by the Hague Protocol.

iii) Montreal convention: The Montreal Convention is formally known as the Convention for the Unification of Certain Rules for International Carriage by Air as a multilateral treaty adopted by a diplomatic meeting of ICAO member states in 1999. It amended important provisions of the Warsaw Convention's regime concerning compensation for the victims of air disasters. The Convention attempts to re-establish uniformity and predictability of rules relating to the international carriage of passengers, baggage and cargo. Whilst maintaining the core provisions which have served the international air transport community for several decades i.e., the Warsaw regime, the new treaty achieves modernization in a number of key areas. It protects passengers by introducing a two-tier liability system that eliminates the previous requirement of proving willful neglect by the air carrier to obtain more than US$75,000 in damages, which should eliminate or reduce protracted litigation.

ICAO has thus 18 annexes to describe and help the functions and standard norms of particular providing air services towards safety and security of Airports, Airlines, Air traffic control, and facilitation even environmental issues. *Those annexes are as below:*

- Annex 1: Personnel Licensing
- Annex 2: Rules of the Air
- Annex 3: Meteorological service and international navigation.
- Annex 4: Aeronautical charts

- Annex 5: Units of measurements to be used in Air and ground operations
- Annex 6: Operation of Aircraft
- Annex 7: Aircraft nationality and Registration Marks
- Annex 8: Airworthiness of Aircraft
- Annex 9: Facilitation
- Annex 10: Aeronautical telecommunication
- Annex 11: Air traffic Services
- Annex 12: Rescue and search operations
- Annex 13: Aircraft accident and incident investigation.
- Annex 14: Aerodromes
- Annex 15: Aeronautical information services
- Annex 16: Environmental Protection
- Annex 17: Security safeguarding international civil aviation against Acts of Unlawful interferences.
- Annex 18: The safe transport of Dangerous goods by Air.

Freedom of Air and Chicago Convention

In 1944, delegates from 52 nations met in Chicago to develop a multilateral treaty securing each nation's rights over its airspace. These "freedoms of the sky" are the fundamental building blocks of air transportation regulation and each subject to specific conditions, such as establishing the frequency of flights or airport usage. There are five basic freedoms that are recognized by virtually all countries. Freedoms 5 and 7 are less common, and typically only negotiated between stalwart trading partners. Freedoms 8 and 9 are only now entering into Air Service Agreements (ASAs), but they are still rare.

The following are the 9 freedoms of Air:

1st freedom: The right to fly over another nation's territory without landing (over flight)
2nd freedom: The right to land in a foreign country for non – traffic reasons, such as maintenance or refueling, without picking up or setting down revenue traffic
3rd freedom: The right to carry traffic (people or cargo) from own State A to treaty partner State B
4th freedom: The right to carry traffic (people or cargo) from treaty partner State B to own State A
5th freedom: The right to carry traffic between two foreign countries with services starting or ending in own State A (i.e. "beyond rights")
6th freedom: The right to carry traffic between two foreign countries via State A. Combines two sets of 3rd and 4th freedom rights as so it is rarely specified explicitly in Air Service Agreements
7th freedom: The right to operate stand-alone services between two foreign states which lie entirely outside A
8th freedom: The right to carry traffic between two points within a foreign state on a service originating or terminating in State A (i.e. consecutive or fill-up sabotage). Example: Alitalia picks up passengers in Atlanta and drops them off in Boston en route to Milan (currently not allowed).
9th freedom: The right to carry traffic between two points within a foreign state with no requirement to originate or terminate in State A (i.e. pure or full sabotage). Example: German-based Air Berlin flies nonstop between London and Manchester without any connection to Germany

Table 1: The 9 freedoms of Air

1.2.3 National Aviation Authority (NAA)

A national aviation authority (NAA) or civil aviation authority is a government statutory authority in each country that oversees the approval and regulation of civil aviation.

The National Aviation Authority (NAA) is the government statutory authority in each country that oversees the approval and regulation of civil aviation.

Due to the inherent dangers in the use of flight vehicles, NAA's typically regulate the following critical aspects of aircraft airworthiness and their operation:

1. Design of aircraft, engines, airborne equipment and ground-based equipment affecting flight safety;
2. Conditions of manufacture and test of aircraft and equipment;
3. Maintenance of aircraft and equipment;
4. Operation of aircraft and equipment;
5. Licensing of pilots and maintenance engineers;
6. Licensing of airports and navigational aids;
7. Standards for air traffic control.

Depending on the legal system of the parent country, the NAA will derive its power from an act of Parliament (such as the Civil or Federal Aviation Act), and is then empowered to make regulations within the bounds of the act. This allows technical aspects of airworthiness to be dealt with by subject matter experts and not politicians.

A NAA may also be involved in the investigation of aircraft accidents, although in many cases this is left to a separate body such as the Australian Transport Safety Bureau (ATSB) in Australia or the National Transportation Safety Board (NTSB) in the United States, to allow independent review of regulatory oversight.

A NAA will regulate the control of air traffic but a separate agency will generally carry out air traffic control functions.

In some countries the national aviation authorities build and operate airports, including non-airside operations such as passenger terminals; the Civil Aviation Authority of the Philippines is one such national authority. In other countries either private companies or local government authorities own and operate individual airports

1.2.4 International Federation of Freight Forwarders Association

International Federation of Freight Forwarders Association (FIATA) was founded on 31th May 1926 in Vienna.

1. FIATA is the largest non-governmental organization in the field of transportation. Its influence is worldwide.

2. FIATA has consultative status with Economic and Social Council (**ECOSOC**) inter alia, United Nations Economic Commission for Europe (UNECE), Economic and Social Commission for Asia and the Pacific (UNESCAP), United Nations Economic and Social Commission for West Asia (ESCWA), United Nations Conference on Trade and Development (UNCTAD), United Nations Commission on International Trade Law (UNCITRAL), etc.

3. FIATA is the recognised representative body of the freight forwarding and logistics industry for – UN & governmental organisations, e.g. International Civil Aviation Organization (ICAO),, Organisation for Economic Co-operation and Development (OECD), World Customs Organization (WCO),

World Bank (WB), World Trade Organization (WTO), etc. – private sector organizations, e.g. Global Shippers' Forum (GSF), International Air Transport Association (IATA), International Criminal Court (ICC), Indefeasible right of use (IRU), etc

FIATA's main objectives are

i) To unite the freight forwarding industry worldwide

ii) To represent, promote and protect the interests of the industry by participating as advisors or experts in meetings of international bodies dealing with transportation

iii) To familiarise trade and industry and the public at large with the services rendered by freight forwarders through the dissemination of information, distribution of publications, etc.

iv) To improve the quality of services rendered by freight forwarders by developing and promoting uniform forwarding documents, standard trading conditions, etc.

v) To assist with vocational training for freight forwarders, liability insurance problems, tools for electronic commerce including electronic data interchange (EDI) and barcode.

In January 2015 International Federation of Freight Forwarders Association (FIATA) represents 110 Association Members in 99 countries 5540 individual Members in 161 countries

Trade facilitation: a matter for collaborative environment

1. As a partner of shippers and carriers the freight forwarder conciliates different interests and needs in the transportation chain, deploying its expertise and market competency.

2. Freight forwarders provide brokerage and assistance in customs, excise, quality assessment, veterinary, phyto-sanitary, safety and security, i.e. de facto full regulatory compliance.
3. Freight forwarders facilitate traders' market access by providing consolidations and trade facilitation services.
4. Freight forwarder and Customs agents fill all possible service requirements of shippers' demand, regardless of modes of transport and compliance domains.

Description of services

"Freight Forwarding and Logistic Services" means services of any kind relating to the carriage performed by single mode or multimodal transport means, consolidation, storage, handling, packing or distribution of the Goods as well as ancillary and advisory services in connection therewith, including but not limited to customs and fiscal matters, declaring the Goods for official purposes, procuring insurance of the Goods and collecting or procuring payment or documents relating to the Goods. Freight Forwarding Services also include logistical services with modern information and communication technology in connection with the carriage, handling or storage of the Goods, and de facto total supply chain management. These services can be tailored to meet the flexible application of the services provided.

Regional and global growth depends on good logistics connectivity and sufficient trade facilitation

i) Trade Facilitation needs a combination of industry good practice and business friendly regulatory environment
ii) Freight forwarders and Customs agents are principal trade facilitators and are working globally

iii) FIATA works to build good practice and facilitation instruments in conjunction with its Association Members

FIATA provides:

- Facilitation through FIATA DOCUMENTS and Model Rules
- Training and awareness programme to enhance knowledge base
- Experienced a consistent advice to UN, regional authorities such as European Union (EU), Asia-Pacific Economic Cooperation (APEC), North American Free Trade Agreement (NAFTA) etc
- Help for governments wishing to improve trade facilitation and logistics connectivity in their countries

FIATA Organisation

FIATA is structured into Institutes, Advisory Bodies, Working Groups and Regional Bodies: Institutes: Airfreight Institute (AFI) Customs Affaires Institute (CAI) Multimodal Transport Institute (MTI) – Working Group Road, Rail and Sea

FIATA Organization has 5 Advisory Bodies:

- Advisory Body of International Affairs (ABIA)
- Advisory Body of Information Technology (ABIT)
- Advisory Body Legal Matters (ABLM)
- Advisory Body Safety and Security (ABSS)
- Advisory Body Vocational Training (ABVT)

FIATA Organization has 4 Regional Bodies:

- Region Africa/Middle East
- Region Americas
- Region Asia/Pacific
- Region Europe Trade Facilitation & FIATA documents

- FIATA has created transport documents and uniform standards and good practice for forwarders worldwide
- Each document with distinctive colour and FIATA logo
- All FIATA documents will be made available electronically.

1.2.5 IATA or FIATA DIALOGUE

The IATA Cargo Agency program has operated for many decades without significant alterations, despite compelling changes in the business relationship between cargo agents and airlines. Today, the traditional IATA Cargo Agent has transitioned from being a selling-agent of the airline to being a purchasing-customer.

In an effort to modernize the current Agency program, FIATA, the International Federation of Freight Forwarders' Association, representing international freight forwarders and logistic providers, and IATA, representing airlines, have joined forces.

The objective of this cooperation is to review, refine, and re-engineer the airline conference based program to one which would be jointly managed by airlines and forwarders. Major steps have been made and this collaboration has resulted in the development of a new joint IATA-FIATA Air Cargo Program, and significant strides in redefining airline and forwarder responsibilities.

The new proposed governance mechanism establishes an IATA-FIATA Governance Board, which recognizes the role played by forwarders in today's marketplace as customers of the airlines, and increases consultations at all levels to achieve common air cargo goals, which are objectives for both FIATA and IATA.

IATA – FIATA Air Cargo Program Frequently Asked Questions (FAQ)

1. Why the need to change now? Despite the successful global operation of the IATA Cargo Agency Program over many decades, the role of IATA Cargo Agents (freight forwarders) has changed. Previously, Cargo Agents were 'selling agents' for and on behalf of airlines. Whereas today, the vast majority of forwarders are 'purchasing customers' of those airlines and their business relationship is often as buyer and seller. To meet the evolving needs of the air cargo industry and better reflect the change in relationships and the transformed role of the freight forwarder, IATA and FIATA joined forces to review, refine, and reengineer the current Cargo Agency Program to develop a new and modernized Program – IATA-FIATA Air Cargo Program (IFACP). This will replace the current IATA Cargo Agency Program. The IFACP will provide a framework of industry standards that are relevant, in line with best practices and safety regulations and fit for purpose. Standards to cover the endorsement of freight forwarders will be administered as a joint program on behalf of and to the benefit of the Participants, in order to ensure that appropriate and relevant standards with respect to cargo operations are developed and maintained

2. How is the new IFACP different to the current IATA Cargo Agency Program? The current Cargo Agency Program set the rules for governing the airline-cargo agent relationship. Its structure reflected the old relationship, where the forwarder was the 'agent' of the airline. This relationship has now evolved. The IFACP reflects the contemporary relationship between freight forwarders

and airlines. The new program moves the decision-making authority regarding the rules of the airline-freight forwarder relationship away from an airline-led conference to a jointly managed and business inspired governance by both forwarders and airlines.

3. What is the benefit of the new IATA-FIATA Air Cargo Program (IFACP)? The structure of the new program better reflects new business models and the buyer-seller relationship that exists today between most forwarders and airlines. By establishing a global joint IATA-FIATA Governance Board (IFGB) and improving joint consultations between the parties also at regional levels, by establishing joint councils, this will ensure Program relevance and as being 'fit-for-purpose'. The parties encourage their respective members to apply the recommended practices on industry initiatives such as those intended to facilitate e-commerce, increase quality, safety and security as will be acknowledged by IFGB. Simplifying the governance structure can reduce the administrative requirement to manage a global program. Properly addressing the principal-to-principal relationship between freight forwarders and airlines will help to diminish the frequency of liability issues.

The Cargo Accounts Settlement System (CASS) continues to be the difficult point in the talks between FIATA and IATA aimed at reaching an agreement on a new Cargo Agent Modernization Programme (CAMP).

The two trade bodies have been working for the past three years or more on modernising the concepts contained in existing IATA provision in this area, reports Lloyd's Loading List.

FIATA has sought seeks a more modern airline-forwarder business relationship for some time to replace the existing CAMPs "after several decades of operation". For years, through the IATA FIATA Consultative Council (IFCC), FIATA had pointed out several issues to be taken up with IATA's Cargo Conferences on repeated occasions, it said in a statement.

"Coming to the present day, FIATA welcomes IATA's initiative to embrace many CAMP agreed principles in today's existing programmes. It is FIATA's desire to continue the dialogue with IATA, a dialogue that must allow FIATA to hold true to its principles, whilst keeping the objective of reaching an agreement in the future, which both parties can accept with confidence that they have served the best interest of the industries they represent.

"After extensive discussions FIATA and IATA were unable to agree on the entire new draft, which contained specific references to IATA's Cargo Accounts Settlement System (CASS) to be integrated into the new programme," the statement added. Forwarders have ensured the success of CASS by allowing an almost 100 per cent payment compliance record, which is openly recognised by the airlines as a resounding achievement.

Forwarders appreciate the efficiency that a collective billing and remittance platform affords. It is however FIATA's view that a forwarder's decision whether to sign up to the CASS Participation

Agreement with IATA, should be made independently by each individual operator, and not be mandated by the FIATA/IATA agreement as a condition to participate. This seemed however a point which IATA was unable to accept on behalf of its constituent airlines.

1.2.6 Federal Aviation Administration (FAA)

The Federal Aviation Administration (FAA) is the national aviation authority of the United States. As an agency of the United States Department of Transportation, it has authority to regulate and oversee all aspects of American civil aviation, Primary Responsibilities,

The responsibilities of the FAA include:

- ❖ Regulating civil aviation to promote safety within the U.S. and abroad;
- ❖ Encouraging and developing civil aeronautics, including new aviation technology;
- ❖ Developing and operating a system of air traffic control and navigation for both civil and military aircraft;
- ❖ Researching and developing the National Airspace System and civil aeronautics;
- ❖ Developing and carrying out programs to control aircraft noise and other environmental effects of civil aviation;
- ❖ Regulating U.S. commercial space transportation. The FAA licenses commercial space launch facilities and private launches of space payloads on expendable launch vehicles.
- ❖ Investigation of aviation incidents, accidents and disasters is conducted by the National Transportation Safety Board (NTSB), an independent US government agency.

Along with the European Aviation Safety Agency (EASA) the FAA is one of the two main agencies world-wide responsible for the certification of aircraft.

Organization of the FAA

FAA is managed by an Administrator, assisted by a Deputy Administrator. Five Associate Administrators report to the

Administrator and direct the line-of-business organizations that carry out the agency's principle functions. The Chief Counsel and nine Assistant Administrators also report to the Administrator. The Assistant Administrators oversee other key programs such as Human Resources, Budget, and System Safety. FAA also has nine geographical regions and two major centers, the Mike Monroney Aeronautical Centre and the William J. Hughes Technical Center.

Key Activities

The FAA's key activities may be summarized as:

i) Safety Regulation

Issuing and enforcing regulations and minimum standards covering manufacturing, operating, and maintaining aircraft; Certification of airmen and airports that serve air carriers.

ii) Airspace and Air Traffic Management

The safe and efficient use of navigable airspace is one of the FAA's primary objectives. The Administration operates a network of airport towers, air route traffic control centers, and flight service stations, as well as developing air traffic rules, assignment of the use of airspace, and the control of air traffic.

iii) Air Navigation Facilities

The FAA builds or installs visual and electronic aids to air navigation, maintains, operates and assures the quality of these facilities as well as sustains other systems to support air navigation and air traffic control, including voice and data communications equipment, radar facilities, computer systems, and visual display equipment at flight service stations.

iv) Civil Aviation Abroad

The FAA promotes aviation safety and encourages civil aviation abroad. It exchanges aeronautical information with foreign authorities, certifies foreign repair shops, airmen, and mechanics, provides technical aid and training, negotiates bilateral airworthiness agreements with other countries and takes part in international conferences.

v) Commercial Space Transportation

The FAA regulates and encourages the U.S. commercial space transportation industry, including licensing commercial space launch facilities and private launches of space payloads on expendable launch vehicles.

vi) Research, Engineering, and Development

The FAA undertakes research on, and development of, the systems and procedures needed for a safe and efficient system of air navigation and air traffic control. The Administration helps develop better aircraft, engines, and equipment and tests or evaluates aviation systems, devices, materials, and procedures. It also undertakes aero medical research.

The FAA's Role in Air Traffic Management

The FAA has a complex set of responsibilities in the Air Traffic Management (ATM). It provides the vast majority of tower-based ATM, including all major airport facilities. It is the sole provider of en-route ATM services in the US. The FAA's service-provision tasks are undertaken by the Air Traffic Organization (ATO), which has been established as a functionally separate entity within the FAA's organizational structure. At the same time, the FAA is responsible for the safety regulation of all US aviation activities, including ATM. For this purpose, an ATM Safety Oversight organization has been established within the regulatory division of the FAA with responsibility for oversight of the safety of the ATO's operations and activities.

1.2.7 European Aviation Safety Agency (EASA)

The European Aviation Safety Agency (EASA) is an agency of the European Union established in 2002 by Regulation (EC) No 216/2008 of the European parliament and the Council in order to ensure a high and uniform level of safety in civil aviation, by the implementation of common safety rules and measures.

EASA has taken over the responsibilities of the former Joint Aviation Authorities (JAA) system which ceased on 30 June 2009. However, it is not a successor agency in legal terms since it functions directly under EU statute. The main difference between EASA and the JAA is that EASA is Regulatory Authority which uses NAAs to implement its Regulations whereas the JAA relied upon the participating NAAs to apply its harmonized codes without having any force of law at source. Since it is self-evidently impossible to create a new Regulatory System 'overnight' EASA has had to accept large parts of the JAA system as its own whilst it develops the new harmonized system required under EU statute.

Mission: EASA states that their mission is to promote the highest common standards of safety and environmental protection in civil aviation.

Remit: The agency's responsibilities are being acquired progressively. In 2008, through the implementation of a new EASA Regulation (EC) No 216/2008, EASA's role was extended beyond its previous scope to cover Flight Operations and Flight Crew Licensing.

In autumn 2009, as part of an aviation package also including the second package of measures for Single European Sky (SES II), the European Community adopted Regulation (EC) No 1108/2009 amending Regulation (EC) No 216/2008 and extending EASA's remit to encompass the field of aerodromes, air traffic management and air navigation services. As previously, however, aircraft used for military, customs and police services, and persons and organizations involved in such activities, remain outside the remit of EASA.

Responsibilities

The agency's responsibilities include:

1. Expert advice to the EU on the drafting new legislation;
2. Developing, implementing and monitoring safety rules, including inspections in the Member States;
3. Type-certification of aircraft and components, as well as the approval of organizations involved in the design, manufacture and maintenance of aeronautical products;
4. Certification of personnel and organizations involved in the operation of aircraft;
5. Certification of organizations providing pan-European ATM/ANS services;
6. Certification of organizations located outside the territory subject to the EC law and responsible for providing ATM/ANS services or ATCO training in the Member States where EC law applies;
7. Authorization of third-country or non EU operators;
8. Safety analysis and research, including publication of an Annual Safety Review.

The Agency's tasks are to:

- ❖ Help the Community legislature draw up common standards to ensure the highest possible levels of safety and environmental protection;
- ❖ Ensure that they are applied uniformly in Europe and that any necessary safeguard measures are implemented;
- ❖ Promote the spread of standards worldwide.

The Agency may adopt various types of act:

It may take binding individual decisions by granting aircraft type certificates and by conducting inspections and investigations; Issue non-binding documents containing certification specifications, acceptable means of compliance and guidance material for use in the certification process and present opinions to the European Commission on the essential requirements and implementing rules to be adopted.

Structure and Governance:

EASA became operational on 28 September 2003 as an independent body of the European Community with its own legal personality. In 2004 the Agency set up its permanent headquarters in Cologne, Germany. It may, with the consent of the Member State concerned, establish local offices in any Member State.

EASA is represented by its Executive Director. The Executive Director alone is empowered to take decisions and adopt acts concerning safety and environmental protection. He decides on inspections and investigations and is the manager of the Agency and, as such, is responsible for preparing and implementing the budget and work programme and for all questions relating to personnel. Since these decisions directly affect people and organizations, the EASA Regulation creates an independent Board of Appeal whose role is to check that the Executive Director has correctly applied European legislation in this field. The Executive Director is appointed by the Agency's Management Board. The Board is responsible for the definition of the Agency's priorities, the establishment of the budget and for monitoring the Agency's operation. It adopts EASA annual report and work programme after approval by the European Commission and the working procedures to be followed by the Agency. The Management Board is composed of one representative of each Member State and one representative of the Commission. The Management Board elects a Chairperson and a Deputy Chairperson from among its members. The term of office is three years and is renewable.

The EASA Advisory Board assists the Management Board in its work. It comprises organizations representing aviation personnel, manufacturers, commercial and general aviation operators, maintenance industry, training organizations and air sports.

The Agency's already employs some 400 professionals from across Europe assigned to several directorates. The core safety related tasks are carried out by the "Rulemaking", "Certification" and "Approvals & Standardization" directorates. The Agency's budget is financed by a contribution from the European Community, fees paid for certificates issued by the Agency and charges for publications and training provided by the Agency.

1.2.8 African Civil Aviation Commission (AFCAC)

African Civil Aviation Commission (AFCAC) The specialized agency of the African Union responsible for Civil Aviation matters in Africa

VISION

To foster a safe, secure, efficient, cost effective, sustainable and environmentally friendly civil aviation industry in Africa.

MISSION

As the specialized Agency of the African Union responsible for Civil Aviation matters in Africa, AFCAC will facilitate cooperation and coordination among African States towards the development of an integrated and sustainable Air transport system; and foster the implementation of ICAO SARPs (Standards And Recommended Practices) and development of harmonized rules and regulations consistent with the best international practices in civil aviation.

VALUES

- Good governance and best practices
- Transparency and accountability
- Professionalism and Integrity
- Safe and just culture

To implement the vision, AFCAC has established five strategic objectives for the period 2011-2016 Strategic Objective:

- ❖ A-Air transport:– Strategic Objective
- ❖ B-Safety:– Strategic Objective
- ❖ C-Security:– Strategic Objective
- ❖ D-Human Resources Development:– Strategic Objective
- ❖ E-Rule of Law:– Technical Cooperation in order to ensure sustainable human resource development for African Aviation, the AFCAC Secretariat organized, coordinated and hosted meetings, courses and seminars in the Technical

fields aimed at the improvement of Aviation Safety in Africa and the development of Human Resources.

The different technical meetings covered deliberations on regional challenges and initiatives, training, lack of adequately trained and skilled personnel, safety of air transport, development of sustainable aviation security, capacity building and need for Government and Industry cooperation, regional and national planning and cooperation.

AFCAC organized many courses to train personnel in Aviation Safety in collaboration with training institutions in order to enhance safety level in conformity with ICAO standards.

AFCAC organized many courses to train personnel in Aviation Safety in collaboration with training institutions in order to enhance safety level in conformity with ICAO standards.

African Civil Aviation Commission Constitution

1. The African Civil Aviation Commission (AFCAC) is an autonomous body and membership shall be open to African States members of African Union (AU).
2. AFCAC is a consultative body and its conclusions and recommendations shall be subject to acceptance by each of the governments.

Objectives

3. The objectives of AFCAC are:

   a. To provide the civil aviation authorities in the Member States with a framework within which to discuss and plan all the required measures of co-ordination and co-operation for all their aviation activities;

b. To promote co-ordination, better utilization and orderly development of African air transport systems.

Functions of AFCAC

4. *The functions of AFCAC shall, in particular, include:*

a. Formulating plans at the regional and sub-regional levels for the operation of air services within and outside Africa;

b. Carrying out studies of the feasibility of standardization of flying equipment and ground units servicing aircraft;

c. Carrying out studies of the possibility of integration of the policies of governments regarding commercial aspects of air transport;

d. Carrying out studies of intra-African fares and rates with a view to adopting a structure conductive to the rapid growth of traffic in Africa;

e. Carrying out studies of regional or sub-regional air transport economic questions other than those mentioned in (b), (c) and (d) above;

f. Encouraging the application of ICAO standards and recommendations on facilitation and supplementing them by further measures aimed at greater facilitation of the movement by air or passengers, cargo and mail;

g. Fostering arrangements between States whenever this will contribute to the implementation of

  ➢ ICAO regional plans for air navigation facilities and services, and

  ➢ ICAO specifications in the fields of airworthiness, maintenance and operation of aircraft, licensing of personnel and aircraft accident investigation.

h. fostering and co-coordinating programmes for the development of existing and future training facilities to cope with the present and future regional and sub-regional requirements for personnel in all fields of civil aviation;

i. Studying the need for collective arrangements for technical assistance in Africa with a view to obtaining the best possible use of all available resources, particularly those provided within the framework of the United Nations Development Programme.

AFCAC shall, in the exercise of its functions, work in close consultation and cooperation with African Union (AU), Economic Commission for Africa (ECA), ICAO and any other governmental or non-governmental international organization concerned with civil aviation.

Organization and Working Arrangements

5. African Civil Aviation Commission (AFCAC) shall meet in ordinary plenary session once every two years.

6. At each ordinary plenary session, AFCAC shall elect its President and four Vice Presidents, one for each sub-region, who will constitute the Bureau of AFCAC.

7. Extraordinary plenary meetings may be convened by the Bureau and must be convened if the Bureau received a request from two – thirds of the AFCAC members.

8. At each ordinary plenary session, AFCAC shall establish its work programme for the period until the following ordinary plenary session.

9. The direction, co-ordination and steering of the work programme between ordinary plenary sessions shall be the responsibility of the Bureau of AFCAC.

10. AFCAC shall determine its own internal organization, arrangements and procedures, including the formation of committees to study special aspects of civil aviation in Africa.

11. Member States should be represented at meetings of AFCAC by delegates senior in rank and competent in the field to be discussed for the authoritative handling of the problems.

12. There shall be established by AFCAC a Secretariat for organizing studies, meetings, maintenance of records and the like. The rules governing the recruitment and conditions of service of the staff shall be determined by AFCAC, ICAO, during the initial period to be determined by AFCAC, shall have the following responsibilities:

    i) To provide staff to carry out studies, organize meetings and undertake related activities;

    ii) To handle minutes, correspondence, etc. ACFAC shall make full use of the experience and assistance of ICAO in conformity with the practice followed by the latter with similar international organizations.

13. At each ordinary plenary session, AFCAC shall prepare and approve a budget of the direct costs of its activities, as indicated in the work programme for the ensuring years. AFCAC shall establish its own financial rules for the assessment of members' contributions and control of expenditure. As regards the indirect costs, these shall be the responsibility of ICAO in accordance with the practice followed by ICAO in the joint financial field .under Chapter XV of the Chicago Convention.

1.3 HANDLING FACILITIES

1.3.1 Airport Handling Procedure (AHP)

It includes several operation like:

- Reservation counter
- Check –in counter
- Baggage Make Up Area (BMA)
- Boarding gate
- Region of aircraft movement and parking (RAMP)
- Arrival Cargo

1.3.2 Aircraft Handling Facilities

The various ground handling services at the airport are as under:

- Ground administration and supervision

    - Representation and liaison services with local authorities
    - Load control, messaging and telecommunications
    - Handling, storage and administration of unit load devices
    - Automation/computer system
    - Any other supervision services before, during or after the flight

- Passenger handling
- Baggage handling
- Freight and mail handling
- Ramp handling:

    - Marshalling of aircraft on the ground at arrival and departure

- Communication between the aircraft and the air-side supplier of services
- Loading and unloading of the aircraft
- Provision and operation of appropriate units for engine starting
- Moving of aircraft at arrival and departure
- Transport, loading on to and unloading from the aircraft of inflight kitchen

- Aircraft services comprising:

  - Fuel and oil handling
  - Aircraft maintenance
  - Flight operations and crew administration
  - Surface transport
  - Catering services
  - Cabin services

Ground Support Equipment Operations

1. Ground support equipment should be operated only by adequate trained, qualified and authorized personnel.
2. Use of portable devices like mobile phones are not permitted while operating the vehicles. Such devices should not be used unless a suitable hands free is available.
3. Equipment should not move across the path of taxiing aircraft or embarking and disembarking passengers. Aircraft and ground personnel should always have the right-of-way.
4. Apron equipment should be positioned behind the equipment restrained line with parking brakes 'ON' prior to the arrival of the aircraft at bay.

5. The passenger loading bridge should be always in fully retracted position prior to the aircraft arrival.
6. During bridge operations only the bridge operator should be in bridgehead. For safety reasons, all other staff should maintain sufficient distance from the bridgehead.
7. Equipment including passenger loading bridges should not move close to the aircraft until it has come to a complete stop, chocks are positioned, engines shut down, and anti-collision beacons switched-off and ground/flight deck contact established.
8. Equipment approaching or leaving the aircraft should not be driven at a high speed.
9. Attachment fittings/transfer bridges and platforms should be correctly deployed. Aerodrome Advisory Circular: Airside Safety Procedure for GH Operation at Airports.
10. Ground equipment with interfaces with the aircraft passenger doors (e.g. passenger steps, catering vehicles, etc.) should have platforms of sufficient width which will allow the aircraft doors to be opened/closed with the equipment in place and the safety rails deployed.
11. Prior to movement of any ground support equipment, a walk around check should be carried out.
12. Hoses and cables on equipment should be properly stowed before the unit is moved.
13. Elevating devices must not be driven in the elevated position except for final positioning.
14. Unserviceable equipment should be clearly tagged 'out of service' and immediately sent for repair.
15. While positioning equipment, care must be exercised to ensure adequate clearance of vehicles, aircraft and other equipment.

16. Standard hand signals must be used to guide ground support equipment. The guide person must be positioned so that clearances can be accurately judged.

17. No vehicle shall be allowed to tow more than six carts, pods, or containers/baggage or pallet dollies at any one time. When left disconnected or parked, all dollies or group of dollies must be left with the parking brakes ON.

18. No vehicle shall be towed by another vehicle unless a suitable tow bar or tow-rope is used for that purpose.

19. The aircraft may be towed only by trained and qualified personnel having airside operations endorsement on their Airport Driving Permit (ADPs). The maximum permitted towing speed shall be 5 kmph.

Passenger Services

+ Incoming passenger acceptance and guidance to baggage claim areas and terminal exit,
+ Lost, damaged and transfer baggage processes of incoming passengers (if any),
+ Outgoing passenger acceptance for flight and baggage processes,
+ Safe acceptance of outgoing passengers to the aircraft,
+ Incoming and outgoing VIP, unaccompanied children and special care passenger services,
+ Specially trained personnel for disabled passengers.

Ramp Services

Ramp services offer the following services with its experienced staff and state of the art technology:

❖ Meeting and marshalling the aircraft,
❖ Offloading and loading the aircraft,

❖ Equipment supply,

❖ Provision of Ground Power Unit, Air Condition Unit and Aircraft Push-Back Tractor services,

❖ Interior cleaning,

❖ Provision of toilet and water services to the aircraft,

❖ De-icing of aircraft in adverse weather conditions and taking measures for anti-icing,

❖ Passenger and crew transport between aircraft and passenger terminals,

❖ Storage of pallets, containers and other unit load devices.

Check-In Counter

Airport check-in uses service counters found at commercial airports handling commercial air travel. The check-in is normally handled by an airline itself or a handling agent working on behalf of an airline. Passengers usually hand over any baggage that they do not wish or are not allowed to carry on to the aircraft's cabin and receive a boarding pass before they can proceed to board their aircraft. Check-in is usually the first procedure for a passenger when arriving at an airport, as airline regulations require passengers to check in by certain times prior to the departure of a flight. This duration spans from 15 minutes to 4 hours depending on the destination and airline. During this process, the passenger has the ability to ask for special accommodations such as seating preferences, inquire about flight or destination information, make changes to reservations, accumulate frequent flyer program miles, or pay for upgrades. The airline check-in's main function, however, is to accept luggage that is to go in the aircraft's cargo hold and issue boarding passes.

Functions of Check-In Counter:

When passenger presents himself/herself at the check-in counter the following checks must be done. Along with that always wish passengers with a pleasant or warm smile and wish the time of the day followed by:

- Check for the security sticker and condition of the baggage. Make sure baggage has been screened and does not contain any dangerous goods articles.
- Request for ticket if not already presented,
- Check ticket details validity of ticket, sector of travel etc.
- Check photo id card of the passenger without any mistake.
- Ask for seat preference.
- Provide assistance according to passenger status which is more active for SSR passengers.
- Weigh baggage and ask about the fragile item.
- Charge for excess baggage only then passenger baggage weight is more than Free Baggage Allowance (FBA).

Issue Boarding Pass and Baggage Tag:

1. Confirm passenger about sector, seat number and baggage.
2. Inform passenger about flight status, gate numbers.

Baggage Make Up Area:

Baggage Make Up Area (BMA) is the adjacent place of terminal building where the check-in/registered baggage are segregated as per flight detail, reconciled by the employee, and consolidated in trolleys and dispatched to the Region of Aircraft Movement and Parking (RAMP). The staff/employee is allocated in the BMA should be vigilant at all time as it is here that a lot of pilferage takes place.

Functions of BMA:

a. Arrange trolleys according to the flights load.
b. Check security sticker of the baggage and segregated as per the destination.
c. Check the types of baggage i.e. hardcase, soft baggage, fragile baggage etc. and then align.
d. Reconcile baggage and load in trolley.
e. Dispatch baggage to aircraft for loading.
f. Inform RAMP staff about trolley count, baggage count and baggage weight.

Boarding Gate/Security Hold Area:

Boarding gate is the place where from passengers move to board the aircraft.

- ❖ Functions of Baggage Gate (BG) or Security Hold Area (SHA):
- ❖ Ensure all passengers' hand baggage tags are stamped.
- ❖ Take details of all SSR passengers before boarding.
- ❖ Inform about boarding of the particular flight.
- ❖ Make announcement from the PA Booth, Passenger Addressing Booth.
- ❖ Reconcile passenger boarding passes.
- ❖ Assist senior citizen passengers, first time traveler, UM (Unaccompanied Minor), mother with infant.
- ❖ Inform RAMP about missing passenger if in case.
- ❖ Pass TOB (Total on Board) to RAMP.
- ❖ Close door within restricted time.

Region of Aircraft Movement and Parking (RAMP)

There is growing realization in the aviation industry that encouraging prompt reporting of issue actually reduces the number of accidents and incidents. An environment of "open reporting" is a key element in fostering "just culture" for the systematic reporting, collection, analysis and dissemination of safety information that will be solely to prevent accidents. Implementation of just culture begins with commitment and action not just by supervisors, managers on the RAMP, they by senior managers as well. Encouraging RAMP personnel to promptly and fully report incidents and accidents is a key element in just culture. RAMP personnel must be trained to view safety as a much more important priority than meeting schedules, and they should be encouraged to report Immediately to their supervisor the slightest scratch or dent in an aircraft any collision between ground equipments and aircraft. So RAMP is the most sensitive area to work. For that staffs need to be more cautious while working.

Functions on Ramp:

- ❖ Take all details like Estimated Time of Arrival (ETA), bay no., incoming load, baggage weight and count, transfer baggage, SSR passengers details etc.
- ❖ Report on the RAMP beforehand for checking Ground Support Equipment (GSE).
- ❖ Announce touchdown.
- ❖ Pass c/on (chocks on) to all department.
- ❖ Aligned stepladder.
- ❖ Evacuate passengers.
- ❖ Ensure anti-sabotage check interior check of cabin by airlines security staff.
- ❖ Offload baggage and cargo.
- ❖ Clean cabin of the aircraft.
- ❖ Load catering.

- ❖ Refueling.
- ❖ Start embarkation.
- ❖ Load outgoing baggage.
- ❖ Tally with boarding gate's employee about exact load.
- ❖ Get the load and trim signed by the captain.
- ❖ Release aircraft.

Ramp Safety:

The following rules apply to all operations on the RAMP: Always be aware of your surroundings. Always wear Personal Protective Equipment (PPE). No smoking. Do not operate any unserviceable vehicles. Keep the RAMP area clear of FOD (Foreign Object Debris). Those who have Airside Driving Permit (ADP), they only operate vehicles.

- ↓ Avoid the intake and exhaust areas of aircraft engines.
- ↓ No vehicles should be parked or driven within 15 meters of a moving aircraft.
- ↓ RAMP equipments must be positioned prior to the arrival of the aircraft behind the restraint line with the parking brakes on.

ARRIVAL:

Functions:

Before arrival of the aircraft the arrival staff must check action on the following items:

- ↓ Review all inbound messages.
- ↓ Check ETA and display the same on the Flight Information Display System (FIDS).
- ↓ Check out aircraft registration and parking Bay.

- Check for any special handling message: VIP/CIP/WCHR/UM. (Where VIP: Very Important Person, CIP: Commercial Important Person, WCHR: Wheel Chair Till RAMP and UM-Unaccompanied Minor.
- Ensure that wheel chair and loaders are available for arrival.
- Arrange for RAMP to RAMP transfer in case Minimum Connection Time (MCT).
- Meet the aircraft and escort passenger to arrival hall.
- Collect all traffic documents from Inflight Manager (IFM).
- Display indicators at the arrival conveyor belt or Carousel. In case of unserviceability of indicators appropriate action must be taken. Fig: – Carousel Belt
- Keep a check on delivery of priority baggage.
- Prepare PIR/DPR (Property Irregularity Report/Damage Property Report).

Property Irregularity Report (PIR) A Property Irregularity Report (PIR) is record of any mishandling of a guests baggage on arrival. This form must be filled in detail and clearly so that the case can be followed up any stuff on duty (SOD). The staff preparing the PIR must sign this form as well as passenger signature. Without this the form cannot be process claims with the insurance company. World Tracer is a SITA/IATA service provided for the tracking of lost or delayed baggage.

1.3.3 Cargo Terminal Facilities

Cargo can be defined as any property which is carried by an aircraft other than mail, company cargo, and engineering equipment and unaccompanied or mishandle baggage.

Consider Ed As Vulnerable In Aviation:

Vast area so surveillance is minimum. Huge number of manpower involved. Mostly cargo terminal is situated outside of the airport area. Sometimes consignment is large to check it property.

Types of Cargo:

Perishable Cargo: Articles of perishable nature, which are liable to perish due to change in climate, temperature, altitude or any other normal exposure inherent to carriage of cargo by air, length of time etc. Example: newspapers, sea food, flowers, medicine.

Valuable/Precious Cargo (VAL): Precious or valuable (VAL) cargo consist of very high value shipments such as currencies, billion, jewelry etc.

Vulnerable Cargo (VUN): This are the shipments, which are vulnerable to theft or pilferage like: cameras, paintings, antiques, watches or parts of watches, electronic goods such as computer and its parts, mobile phones, pagers, other expensive electronic goods.

Live Animals (AVI): Only animals, which are appear to be in good health and condition, should be accepted for carriage by air. The cages/Boxes having the livestock/animals should be examined to ensure that they do not contain anything which is dangerous to the safety of the aircraft.

Human Remains (HUM): As per the cargo technology human remains are the dead body of human being. The required identification and document as enumerated below death certificate, embalming certificate, police clearance and identity of relatives.

Bonded Cargo: All cargos which are customs cleared are called as bonded cargo. All cargos which are used for exporting is called as bonded cargos.

Inbound Bonded Cargo: If the bonded cargo is coming from an international sector and connected to domestic flight as an airside transfer from international warehouse to the domestic side, then the cargo will be accepted after checking the documents.

Company Cargo: There may be a requirement of transporting stores of the company from one place to other in aircraft. These, moved as company stores must be subjected to security checks applicable to company mails. This could either be in the form of x-rays or physical checks.

Aog Spares Cargo: AOG refers to Aircraft on Ground, which implies that the aircraft has been grounded due to some technical snag. There would be a requirement of transporting aircraft spares as replacement urgently to the affected station where the aircraft has been grounded.

Cargo and Mail Services

- Acceptance of export cargo and mail documents,
- Physical control and preparation of export cargo and mail,
- Monitoring cargo and mail for proper loading to the aircraft,
- Custom transactions of export cargo,
- Detection of disruption of imported cargo and mail if any, and taking necessary actions,
- Completion of custom clearance of the imported cargo and preparing it for delivery to recipients,
- Notification of recipients,
- Transfer cargo services.

- ❖ Load Control, Communications And Flight Operation Services
- ❖ Load Control and Communications Services
- ❖ Coordination of aircraft servicing units,
- ❖ Preparation and distribution of flight documents such as customs declaration, loading instruction, load sheet, manifest, weather forecast, flight plan etc,
- ❖ Load control, weight and balance calculations,
- ❖ Transmission and reception of all operational messages, notification of all related units,
- ❖ Communication and coordination between aircraft and ground services.

1.3.4 Custom Clearance Process

Customs is an authority or agency in a country responsible for collecting and safeguarding customs duties and for controlling the flow of goods including animals, transports, personal effects and hazardous items in and out of a country. Depending on local legislation and regulations, the importer export of some goods may be restricted or forbidden, and the customs agency enforces these rules.

In all International Airports, the passenger has the option of seeking clearance through the Green Channel or through the Red Channel subject to the nature of goods being carried. For the purpose of Customs clearance of arriving passengers, a two channel system has been adopted:

i) *Green Channel for passengers not having any dutiable goods.*
ii) *Red Channel for passengers having dutiable goods.*

Passengers walking through the Green Channel with prohibited goods are liable to prosecution or penalty and confiscation of goods. Trafficking of Narcotics and Psychotropic substances is a serious offence and is punishable with imprisonment.

Customs clearance work involves preparation and submission of documentations required to facilitate export or imports into the country, representing client during customs examination, assessment, payment of duty and co taking delivery of cargo from customs after clearance along with documents.

Some of the documents involved in customs clearance are:

Exports Documentation: Exports documents are Purchase order from Buyer, Sales Invoice, Packing List, Shipping bill, Bill of Lading or air way bill, Certificate of Origin and any other specific documentation as specified by the buyer, or as required by financial institutions or as per importing country regulations.

Imports Documentation: Purchase Order from Buyer, Sales Invoice of supplier, Bill of Entry, Bill of Lading or Air way bill, Packing List, Certificate of Origin, and any other specific documentation required by the buyer, or financial institution or the importing country regulation.

The rules, regulations, and laws are a bit different from country to country, sometimes from port to port within a country, making someone who specializes in customs clearance very important to a shipper exporting and importing goods.

These specialists are called customs brokers and the work they do is called customs brokerage or sometimes customs broking. Having the wrong person handle the customs brokerage can be very problematic. Shipping containers are warehoused as they go through customs clearance. Warehousing and storage fees can add up quickly.

Conclusion

The transport of commercial cargo is a key economic indicator of international trade and the state of the global economy. Air cargo airlines and airlines which carry a portion of freight traffic contribute to the larger courier service industry, which, simply put, delivers messages, packages, and mail. Air freight is a small portion of a much larger logistics networks which involve production, packaging, material handling, inventory, transportation, warehousing, security, and information flow.

Chapter 2

World Geography

Introduction

What Is Geography? Geography is the spatial study of the earth's surface (from the Greek geo, which means "Earth," and graphein, which means "to write"). Geographers study the earth's physical characteristics, its inhabitants and cultures, phenomena such as climate, and the earth's place within the universe. Geography examines the spatial relationships between all physical and cultural phenomena in the world. Geographers also look at how the earth, its climate, and its landscapes are changing due to cultural intervention.

The first known use of the word geography was by Eratosthenes of Cyrene (modern-day Libya in North Africa), an early Greek scholar who lived between 276 and 194 BCE. He devised one of the first systems of longitude and latitude and calculated the earth's circumference. Additionally, he created one of the first maps of the world based on the available knowledge of the time. Around the same time, many ancient cultures in China, southern Asia, Polynesia, and the Arabian Peninsula also developed maps and navigation systems used in geography and cartography.

Geography is a much broader field than many people realize. Most people think of area studies as the whole of geography. In reality, geography is the study of the earth, including how human activity has changed it. Geography involves studies that are much broader than simply understanding the shape of the earth's landforms. Physical geography involves all the planet's physical systems. Human geography incorporates studies of human culture, spatial relationships, interactions between humans and the environment, and many other areas of research that involve the different subspecialties of geography.

We live in a world of amazing beauty, infinite complexity and rigorous challenge. Geography is the subject which opens the door to this dynamic world and prepares each one of us for the role of global citizen in the 21st century.

World Geography is an important part of Travel & Tourism Industry. Any travel professional who handles the matters related to preparations of:

1. *Itineraries,*
2. *Reservations,*
3. *Group Bookings,*
4. *Fare calculations and*

Ticketing should have knowledge about the world geography and also should be able to identify the cities by the location, country, areas and sub areas defined by IATA. Geography is a subject which builds on young people's own experiences, helping them to formulate questions, develop their intellectual skills and prepares into handling every type of travel client. If a person who is related to travel field is having the knowledge about the world geography then he or she can easily plan out the best suitable itinerary for their clients. The Eastern Hemisphere and the Western Hemisphere which are the two parts of the world as per the elementary geography is further divided by IATA into

3 traffic conference areas called IATA Areas or TC1, TC2 and TC3 which comprise of further sub areas and that is different from the geographical definitions.

World regional geography studies various world regions as they compare with the rest of the world. Factors for comparison include both the physical and the cultural landscape. The main questions are who lives there? What are their lives like? What do they do for a living? Physical factors of significance can include location, climate type, and terrain. Human factors include cultural traditions, ethnicity, language, religion, economics, and politics. World regional geography focuses on regions of various sizes across the earth's landscape and aspires to understand the unique character of regions in terms of their natural and cultural attributes. Spatial studies can play an important role in regional geography. The scientific approach can focus on the distribution of cultural and natural phenomena within regions as delimited by various natural and cultural factors. The focus is on the spatial relationships within any field of study, such as regional economics, resource management, regional planning, and landscape ecology.

Geographic skills provide the necessary tools and technologies for thinking geographically. These skills help people make important decisions in their daily lives, such as how to get to work and where to shop, vacation, or go to school. They also help people make reasoned political decisions and aid in the development and presentation of effective, persuasive arguments for and against matters of public policy. All of these decisions involve the ability to acquire, arrange, and use geographic information.

2.1 TRAFFIC CONFERENCE

Divisions of the world used for the purposes of fare construction. There are three traffic conference areas (TCs): TC1 comprises North and South America; TC2 comprises Europe, Africa, and the Middle East; TC3 comprises Asia and the Pacific. Any of the three IATA world-wide subdivisions used by the airline industry (aviation, travel)

According to **International Air Transport Association (IATA) World geography has:**

- Traffic Conference-1 Sub-Areas,
- Traffic Conference-2 Sub-Areas and
- Traffic Conference-3 Sub-Areas.

IATA has divided world into three areas: TC1, TC2, TC3.

- TC1 is Known as Western Hemisphere,
- TC2 and TC3 are together known as Eastern Hemisphere.

IATA/World Travel Geography

All the airlines of the world operate their services to hundreds of destinations in different countries for the travelers to visit for varieties of purposes. Airlines focus upon their network of destinations in their advertisements as each of those is a valuable product for marketing and selling.

Geography is one of the key aspects in planning and pricing of a travel. Importantly, IATA has divided the world in its Traffic conference areas and further sub areas with some exceptions to the general political geography which is particularly applied to various international air tariff construction rules.

Each traveler or customer may need to travel to a different destination or a set of destinations. He contacts a travel consultant in expectation of an expert advice regarding the features of the destinations he likes to visit and the best way his travel plan is routed through. Therefore, it is extremely essential for a travel consultant to have substantial knowledge of world destination geography

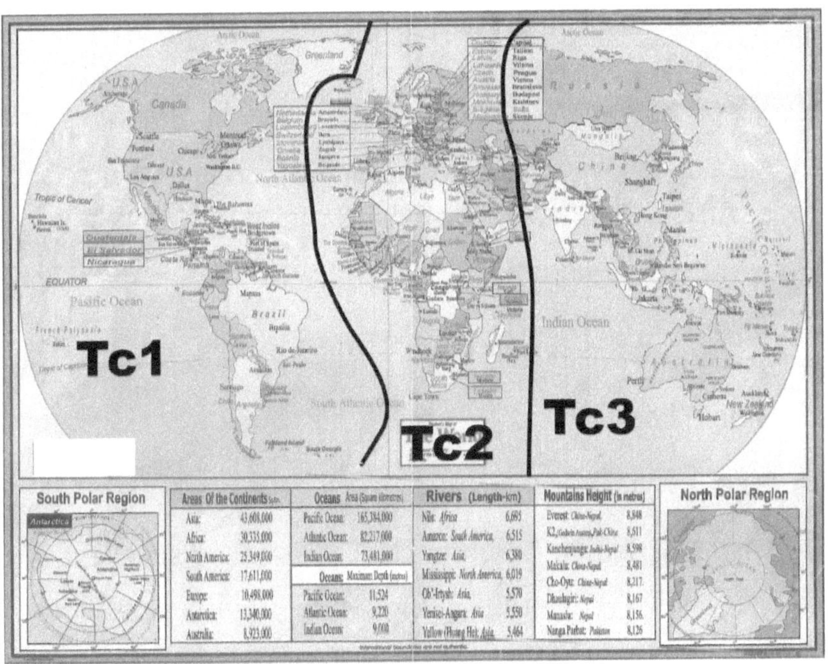

Figure 1: Traffic Conferences,
Source: travelconsultantsskills.blogspot.com/

IATA Area 1 or TC 1

IATA Area 1 or TC 1 comprises of North America, South America, Central America and the adjacent islands like Greenland, Bermuda, West Indies, Islands of the Caribbean Sea, Hawaiian Islands which includes Midway and Palmyra.

Traffic Conference: 1 Sub-Areas. TC1 – North Atlantic

North Atlantic comprises of Canada, Greenland, USA and Mexico excluding Alaska, Hawaii, Puerto Rico and US Virgin Island.

TC 1 – Mid Atlantic, Including The Caribbean Islands, Central America, South America plus Panama Canal Zone except Argentina, Brazil, Chile, Paraguay and Uruguay. TC 1 – South Atlantic, Argentina, Brazil, Chile, Paraguay & Uruguay.

IATA Area 2 or TC2

IATA Area 2 or Traffic Conference (TC) area 2 comprises of Europe, Africa and Ascension Island and parts of Asia west of Ural Mountains including Iran and countries of Middle East

1. Europe
2. Africa
3. Middle East

IATA Area 3 or TC3

IATA Area 3 or Traffic Conference (TC) area 3 Asia (East of the Urals), Oceania, (Australia, New Zealand and South Pacific Islands)

1. South East Asia
2. South Asian Sub continent
3. Japan and Korea (Japkor)
4. South West pacific

North Atlantic: includes: Greenland, Canada, USA includes Alaska and Hawaiian island, Mexico, Puerto and the Virgin Island and St Pierre and the Miquelon

2.2 TIME DIFFERENCES

From east to west they are Atlantic Standard Time (AST), Eastern Standard Time (EST), Central Standard Time (CST), Mountain Standard Time (MST), Pacific Standard Time (PST), Alaskan Standard Time (AKST), Hawaii-Aleutian Standard Time (HST), Samoa standard time (UTC-11) and Chamorro Standard Time (UTC+10)

2.3 LONGITUDE AND LATITUDE

The equator is the largest circle of latitude on Earth. The equator divides the earth into the Northern and Southern Hemispheres and is called 0 degrees latitude. The other lines of latitude are numbered from 0 to 90 degrees going toward each of the poles. The lines north of the equator toward the North Pole are north latitude, and each of the numbers is followed by the letter "N." The lines south of the equator toward the South Pole are south latitude, and each of the numbers is followed by the letter "S." The equator (0 latitude) is the only line of latitude without any letter following the number. Notice that all lines of latitude are parallel to the equator, they are often called parallels, and that the North Pole equals 90 degrees N and the South Pole equals 90 degrees S.

Noted parallels include both the Tropic of Cancer and the Tropic of Capricorn, which are 23.5 degrees from the equator. At 66.5 degrees from the equator are the Arctic Circle and the Antarctic Circle near the North and South Pole, respectively.

Meridians or Lines of Longitude

The prime meridian sits at 0 degrees longitude and divides the earth into the Eastern and Western Hemispheres. The prime meridian is defined as an imaginary line that runs through the

Royal Observatory in Greenwich, England, a suburb of London. The Eastern Hemisphere includes the continents of Europe, Asia, and Australia, while the Western Hemisphere includes North and South America. All meridians (lines of longitude) east of the prime meridian (0 and 180) are numbered from 1 to 180 degrees east (E); the lines west of the prime meridian (0 and 180) are numbered from 1 to 180 degrees west (W). The 0 and 180 lines do not have a letter attached to them. The meridian at 180 degrees is called the International Date Line. The International Date Line (180 degrees longitude) is opposite the prime meridian and indicates the start of each day (Monday, Tuesday, etc.). Each day officially starts at 12:01 a.m., at the International Date Line. Do not confuse the International Date Line with the prime meridian (0 longitude). The actual International Date Line does not follow the 180-degree meridian exactly. A number of alterations have been made to the International Date Line to accommodate political agreements to include an island or country on one side of the line or another.

Climate and Latitude

The earth is tilted on its axis 23.5 degrees. As it rotates around the sun, the tilt of the earth's axis provides different climatic seasons because of the variations in the angle of direct sunlight on the planet. Places receiving more direct sunlight experience a warmer climate. Elsewhere, the increased angle of incoming solar radiation near the earth's poles results in more reflected sunlight and thus a cooler climate. The Northern Hemisphere experiences winter when sunlight is reflected off the earth's surface and less of the sun's energy is absorbed because of a sharper angle from the sun.

Latitude and longitude are imaginary or unreal lines drawn on maps to easily locate places on the Earth. Latitude is distance north or south of the equator, an imaginary circle around the Earth halfway between the North Pole and the South Pole and longitude is distance east or west of the prime meridian, an imaginary line running from north to south through Greenwich, England. Both are measured in terms of the 360 degrees symbolized by ° of a circle. The Equator is the line of 0° latitude, the starting point for measuring latitude. The latitude of the North Pole is 90° N, and that of the South Pole is 90° S. The latitude of every point in between must be some degree north or south, from 0° to 90°. One degree of latitude covers about 69 miles 111 kilometers.

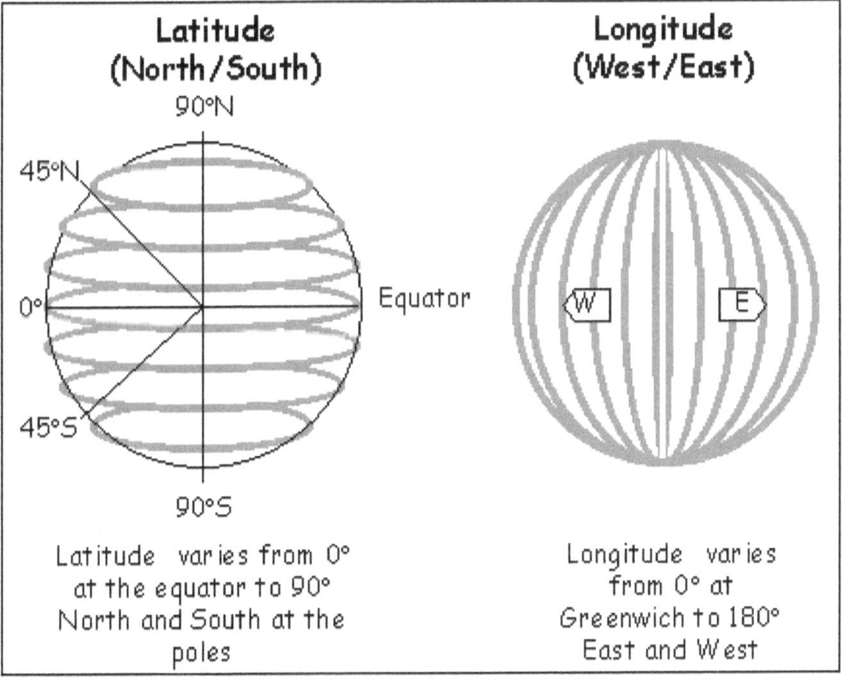

Figure 2: Longitude and Latitude

Longitude is measured in degrees east or west of the prime meridian. This means one half of the world is measured in degrees of east longitude up to 180°, and the other half in degrees of west longitude up to 180°. See the diagrams below to understand latitudes and longitudes better.

Latitude and Longitude are the units that represent the *coordinates at geographic coordinate system.* Just like every actual house has its address which includes the number, the name of the street, city, etc, every single point on the surface of earth can be specified by the *latitude and longitude coordinates.* Therefore, by using latitude and longitude we can specify virtually any point on earth.

The **latitude** has the symbol of *phi*, and it shows the angle between the straight line in the certain point and the equatorial plane. The latitude is specified by degrees, starting from 0° and ending up with 90° to both sides of the equator, making latitude Northern and Southern. The equator is the line with 0° latitude. The **longitude** has the symbol of lambda and is another angular coordinate defining the position of a point on a surface of earth. The longitude is defined as an angle pointing west or east from the Greenwich Meridian, which is taken as the Prime Meridian. The longitude can be defined maximum as 180° east from the Prime Meridian and 180° west from the Prime Meridian.

Both **latitude and longitude** are measured in **degrees**, which are in turn divided into minutes and seconds. For example, the tropical zone which is located to the south and to the north from the Equator is determined by the limits of 23°26'13.7" S and 23°26'13.7" N. Or. For example, the geographical coordinates of the mount Ngauruhoe in New Zealand, famous with its being the filming area for the Lord of the Rings movie, has the geographic coordinates of 39°09'24.6"S 175°37'55.8"E

2.4 GREENWICH MEAN TIME (GMT) AND UTC

Mean solar time at the village of Greenwich near London which, as decided at the International Meridian Congress of 1884, is assigned 0 degrees longitude (called Prime Meridian). Because it is based on the Earth's rotation (which is irregular) it actually follows a fictitious Mean Sun that moves at a uniform speed along the equator. A 19th century worldwide time standard, it was replaced in 1970 by the Coordinated Universal Time (UTC) for astronomical and navigational use, but is still in common use by airlines and radio and television stations.

Time Zones

Universal Time (UT), Coordinated Universal Time (UTC), Greenwich Mean Time (GMT), or Zulub Time (Z): all four terms can be defined as local time at 0 degrees longitude, which is the prime meridian (location of Greenwich, England). This is the same time under which many military operations, international radio broadcasts, and air traffic control systems operate worldwide. UTC is set in zero – to twenty-four-hour time periods, as opposed to two twelve-hour time periods (a.m. and p.m.). The designations of a.m. and p.m. are relative to the central meridian: a.m. refers to ante meridiem, or "before noon," and p.m. refers to post meridiem, or "after noon." UT, UTC, GMT, and Z all refer to the same twenty-four-hour time system that assists in unifying a common time in regard to global operations. For example, all air flights use the twenty-four-hour time system so the pilots can coordinate flights across time zones and around the world.

Greenwich Mean Time (GMT) and all of the world's time is set from Greenwich in London, the site of the Millennium Dome. Those countries to the east of London are ahead of us time as the earth spins from day to night. Those countries on the west of London are behind in time.

The Difference between GMT and UTC

Greenwich Mean Time (GMT) is often interchanged or confused with Coordinated Universal Time (UTC). But GMT is a time zone and UTC is a time standard, Although GMT and UTC share the same current time in practice, there is a basic difference between the two:

- GMT is a time zone officially used in some European and African countries. The time can be displayed using both the 24-hour format (0 – 24) or the 12-hour format (1 – 12 am/pm).
- UTC is not a time zone, but a time standard that is the basis for civil time and time zones worldwide. This means that no country or territory officially uses UTC as a local time

UTC, GMT and Daylight Saving Time

Neither UTC nor GMT ever change for Daylight Saving Time (DST). However, some of the countries that use GMT switch to different time zones during their DST period.

2.5 CALCULATION OF TOTAL TRANSPORTATION TIME

Transport cost includes not only monetary cost but also time cost. Time cost is not directly Measurable.

Development of transport technologies improve the productivity of transport industry, which are in large part due to reduction of transport time through increase in speed.

Reduction of transport time has great benefit on the economy: transport firms (carriers) save labor and capital costs; manufacturing firms (shippers) increase the value of their products; consumers enjoy fast delivery (e.g., increasing availability of fresh foods produced in distant locations). In longer term, these benefits would be enhanced by modifying the ways of organizing economic activities; changes in location of firms, reorganization of supply chain network, introducing more elaborate logistics (e.g., just-in-time system), etc.

The problem of minimization of the total transportation cost is commonly treated in literature as a basic single objective linear transportation model. The transportation time is relevant in a variety of real transportation problems, too. There are two types of problems regarding the transportation time (i) minimization of the total transportation time (linear function, as aggregate the products of transportation time and quantity), called minimization of 1st transportation time, and (ii) minimization of the transportation time of the longest active transporting route (nonlinear function), called minimization of second transportation time. For (ii), the total number of units on transportation operation with longest time is minimized in. An important variant of the total transportation time problems is formulated and resolved in which are on whole included in. The transportation time of the longest active transportation route(s) in problems where all destinations do not have the same importance are analyzed as the three classes single criteria and multi criteria problems of the transportation time.

2.6 AIRPORT 3-LETTER CODES

The International Air Transport Association's (IATA) Location Identifier, a unique 3-letter code, is used in aviation to identify mainly locations of airports throughout the world.

TC I SUB AREA 1

Country City City Code

Greenland Nuuk GOH

Canada (11 Major cities)

Vancouver YVR

Montreal YMQ

Ottawa YOW

Toronto YTO

Edmonten YEA

Calgary YYC

Regine YRG

Winnipeg YWG

Halifax YHZ

St John YYT

Quebec YQB

Alaska Anchorage ANU

USA (25 Major cities)

Detroit DDT

Chicago CHI

Boston BOS

New York NYC

Washington WAS

San Francisco SFO

Los Angeles LAX

Dallas DAL

Atlanta ATL

Miami MIA

Seattle SEA

Phoenix PHX

Las Vegas LAS

Boise BOI

Salt lake city SLC

Denver DEN

New orlando MCO

Philadelphia PHL

Pittsburgh PIT

Cincinnati CVG

Indiana polis IND

Minneapolis MSP

St Louis STL

New Orleans MSY

Houston HOU

3. Hawaiian island Honolulu **HNL**

4. Mexico 3 Major cities Mexico city MEX

Acapulco ACA

Guadalajara GDL

5. Puerto Rico and the virgin islands san Juan SJU

6. St Pierre and the Miquelon

Sub area 2 Mild Atlantic 15 countries

Belize Belmopan BCV

Guatemala Guatemala city GUA

El Salvador San Salvador SAL

Honduras Tegucigalpa TGU

Nicaragua Managua MGA

Costa Rica San Jose SJO

Panama Panama city PTY

Colombia Bogotá BOG

Venezuela Caracas CCS

Guyana St George GEO

Surname Paramaribo PBM

French Guiana cayenne CAY

Ecuador Quito UIO

Guayaquil GYE

Peru Lima LIM

Bolivia Lapaz LPB

Sub area 3

Argentina Buenos Aires BUE

Brazil Brasilia BSB

Sao Paulo SAO

Rio De Janeiro RIO

Recife REC

Chile Santiago De Chile SCL

Paraguay Asuncion ASU

Uruguay Montevideo MVD

2. CARRIBEAN ISLANDS

Anguilla

Antigua And Barbuda St Johns ANU

Aruba

Bahamas Nassau NAS

Barbados Bridge Town BGI

Bermuda Hamilton BDA

Cuba Havana HAV

Cayman Islands

Dominica Roseau DOM

Dominican Republic Santo Domingo SDQ

French Guyana

Guadeloupe

Grenada St George's GND

Haiti Port Au Prince PAP

Jamaica Kingston KIN

Monte Serret

Martinique

Netherland Antilles

St Kits And Nevis Basseterre SKB

St Lucia Castries SLU

Trinidad And Tobago Port Of Spain POS

St Vincent And The Grenadines Kingstown SVD

Turks And Cairos islands

The Virgins Island British (UK)

TRAFFIC CONFERENCE II

Sub area 1: EUROPE 46 COUNTRIES

Norway Oslo OSL

Sweeden Stock Holm STO

Danmark Copen Hagen CPH

Finland Helsinki HEL

Russia Moscow MOW

St peterbough LED

Estonia Tallin TLL

Lativia Riga RIX

Lithuania Vilnius VNO

Beralus Minsk MSQ

Ukraine Kiev IEV

Moldova Chisinau KIV

Romania Bucharest BUH

Bulgaria Sofia SOF

Turkey Istambul IST

Ankara ANK

Greece Athens ATH

Thessaloniki SKG

Cyprus Nicosia NIC

Larnaca LCA

Iceland Reykjavik REK

Ireland Dublin DUB

UNITED KINGDOM London LON

Birmingham BHX

Manchester MAN

Edinburg EDI

Glasgow GLA

Belfast BFS

Portugal Lisbon LIS

Oporto OPO

Faro FAO

Spain Madrid MAD

Malaga AGP

Barcelona BCN

France Paris PAR

Lyon LYS

Marseilles MRS

Nice NCE

Luxembourg Luxembourg LUX

Belgium Brussels BRU

Antwerp ANR

Netherland Amsterdam AMS

Rotterdam RTM

Germany Berlin BER

Hamburg HAM

Dusseldorf DUS

Frankfurt FRA

Munich MUC

Poland Warsaw WAW

Italy Rome ROM

Milan MIL

Venice VCE

Naples NAP

Switzerland Berne BRN

Geneva GVA

Zurich ZRH

Austria Vienna VIE

Innsbruck INN

Czeck republic Prague PRG

Slovakia Bratislava BTS

Slovenia Ljubljana LJU

Hungary Budapest BUD

Serbia Belgrade BEG

Kosovo pristine PTN

Macedonia Skopje SKP

Albania Tirana TIA

Montenegro podgorico TGD

Bosnia Sarajevo SJJ

Croatia Zagreb CRZ

Malta Valletta MLA

Tunisia Tunis TUN

Algeria Algiers ALG

Morocco Casablanca CAS

Rabat RBA

Marrakesh RAK

Gibraltar Gibraltar GIB

Andorra

Monaco

San Marino

Liechtenstein

Sub area 2 Middle East

Yemen Sanaa SAA

Oman Muscat MCT

Qatar Doha DOH

Egypt Cairo CAI

Alexandria ALY

Saudi Arabia Riyadh RUH

Jeddhah JED

UAE Dubai DXB

Abudhabi AUH

Sharajah SHJ

Sudan Khartoum KRT

Israel Jerusalem JRS

Tel Aviv TLV

Syria Damascus DAM

Bahrain Manama HAH

Iraq Baghdad BGW

Iran Tehran THR

Kuwait Kuwait KWT

Jordan Amman AMM

Lebanon Beirut BEY

SUB AREA 3 AFRICA

EASTERN AFRICA

Rwanda Kigali KGL

Eritrea Asmara ASM

Djibouti Djibouti JIB

Ethiopia Addis Ababa ADD

Kenya Nairobi NBO

Mombasa MBA

Uganda Entebbe EBB

Burundi Bujumbura BJM

Tanzania Dodoma DOD

Dal-es-salaam DAR

Southern Africa

Mozambique Maputo MPM

Swaziland Mbabane MTS

Lesotho Maseru MSU

South Africa Pretoria PRY

Johannesburg JNB

Cape Town CPT

Botswana Gaborone GBE

Namibia Windnock WDH

Angola Luanda LAD

Central Africa

Zambia Lusaka LUN

Zimbabwe Harare HRE

Malawi Lilongwe LLW

Western Africa Western Sahara

Mauritania Nouakchott NKC

Mali Bamako BKO

Niger Niamey NIM

Chad Ndjamena NDJ

Nigeria Abuja ABV

Logos LOS

Central Africa republic Bangwi BGF

RD Congo Kinshasa FIH

Brazzaville BZV

Gabon Libreville LBV

Cameroon Yaoundé YAO

Douala DLA

Equatorial guinea Malabo SSG

Benin Cotonou COO

Togo Rome LFW

Ghana Accra ACC

Ivory Coast Yamoussoukro ASK

Abidjan ABJ

Burkinafaso Ouagadougou OUA

Liberia Monrovia MLW

Sierra Leone Freetown FNA

Guinea Conakry CKY

Guinea Bissau Bissau OXB

Gambia Banjul BJL

Senegal Dakar DKR

Sao Tome Principe Sao Tome TMS

Indian ocean islands Seychelles Victoria SEZ

Comoros

Mayotte

Re – union

Mauritius Port Louis MRU

Madagascar Antananarivo TNR

Libya Tripoli TIP

TRAFFIC CONFERENCE III

Sub area 1 South East Asia

Mongolia Ulan Batar ULN

Kazakhstan Astana TSE

Almaty ALA

Uzbekistan Tashkent TAS

Kyrgyzstan Bishkek FRU

Tajikistan Dushambe DYU

Twikmenistan Ashgabat ASB

Georgia Tibilisi TBS

Armenia Yerevan EVN

Azerbaijan Baku BAK

China Beijing BJS

Shanghai SHA

Hong Kong Hong Kong HKG

Taiwan Chinese Taiper TPE

Brunei Bandar Seri Begawan BWN

Cambodia Phnom Penh PNH

Timor Leste Dili DIL

Indonesia Jakarta JKT

Laos Vientiane VTE

Malaysia Kualalumpur KUL

Singapore Singapore SIN

Russia East Of The Arabs Khabarov Sk KHV

Philippines Manila MNL

Thailand Bangkok BKK

Vietnam Hanoi HAN

Ho Chimink City SGN

Myanmar Yangon RGN

Sub area 2 south Asian sub – continents

Afghanistan Kabul KBL

Pakistan Islamabad ISB

Karachi KHI

Nepal Katmandu KTM

Bhutan Paro PBH

Maldives Male MLE

Srilanka Colombo CMB

Bangladesh Dhaka DAC

India Delhi DEL

Mumbai BOM

Chennai MAA

Kolkata CCU

Hyderabad HYD

Sub Area 3 JAPAN AND KOREA

North Korea Pyongyang FNJ

South Korea Seoul SEL

Japan Tokyo TYO

Osaka OSA

Nagoya NGO

Sub Are 4 South West Pacific

Palau Koror ROR

Papua New Guinea Port Moresby POM

Australia Canberra CBR

Sydney SYD

Perth PER

Darwin DRW

Melbourne MEL

Brisbane BNE

Adelaide ADL

Tasmania Hobart HBA

New Zealand Wellington WLG

Christ Church CHC

Auckland AKL

Marshall Islands Majuro MAJ

Northern Mariana Islands

Micronesia

Salomon Islands Honiara HIR

New Caledonia Noumea NOU

Vanuatu Pot Vila VLI

Tuvalu Funafuti FUN

Fiji Islands Suva SUV

Nadi NAN

Nauru Yeren INU

Tonga Nuuk Alofa TBU

French Polynesia Papute PPT

Cook Islands

Samoa Apia APW

American Samoa Fagatogo PPG

Kiribati Tarawa TRW

Wallis Futana Mata' Utu FUT

Table 2: Airport 3-Letter Codes

AIRLINE 2 – LETTER CODES

Major Airline Code List

	Airline	Country	Carrier Code
1.	American Airlines Inc.	U.S.A.	AA
2.	Air Canada	CANADA	AC
3.	Alitalia-Compagnia Aerea Italiana	S.P. ITALY	AZ
4.	Air France	FRANCE	AF
5.	Air Caledonie International	CALEDONIA	SB
6.	Air New Zealand Ltd.	NEW ZEALAND	NZ
7.	Air India Ltd.	INDIA	AI
8.	Aeromexico	MEXICO	AM
9.	All Nippon Airways Co., Ltd.	JAPAN	NH
10.	Air Tahiti Nui	TAHITI	TN

11.	Austrian Airlines Ag	AUSTRIA	OS
12.	Air Pacific	FIJI	FJ
13.	Ahk Air Hong Kong Ltd.	HONG KONG	LD
14.	Aeroflot Russian Airlines	RUSSIA	SU
15.	Air Niugini Pty Ltd.	NIUGINI	PX
16.	Air Nippon Co., Ltd.	JAPAN	EL
17.	Asiana Airlines Inc.	KOREA	OZ
18.	Air China Ltd.	CHINA	CA
19.	British Airways P.L.C.	U.K.	BA
20.	Continental Airlines, Inc.	U.S.A.	CO
21.	Cathay Pacific Airways Ltd.	CHINA	CX
22.	Cargolux Airlines Int'l S.A.	LUXEMBURG	CV
23.	China Airlines Ltd	TAIWAN	CI
24.	China Eastern Airlines	CHINA	MU
25.	China Southern Airlines	CHINA	CZ
26.	Delta Air Lines, Inc.	U.S.A.	DL
27.	Dalavia Far East Airways	RUSSIA	H8
28.	Egyptair	EGYPT	MS
29.	Emirates Sky Cargo	U.A.E.	EK
30.	Eva Airways Corp.	TAIWAN	BR
31.	Fedex	U.S.A.	FX
32.	Finnair O/Y	FINLAND	AY
33.	Garuda Indonesia	INDONESIA	GA
34.	Hong Kong Dragon Airlines Limited.	HONG KONG	KA
35.	Iran-Air	IRAN	IR
36.	Japan Airlines Co. Ltd	JAPAN	JL
37.	Japan Asia Airways Co., Ltd.	JAPAN	EG
38.	KLM Royal Dutch Airlines	NETHERLANDS	KL
39.	Korean Air Lines Co.,Ltd.	KOREA	KE
40.	Lufthansa Cargo Ag.	GERMANY	LH
41.	Malaysia Airlines System Berhad	MALAYSIA	MH

42.	Miat-Mongolian Airlines	MONGOLIA	OM
43.	Northwest Airlines, Inc.	U.S.A.	NW
44.	Nippon Cargo Airlines	JAPAN	KZ
45.	Philippine Airlines, Inc.	PHILIPPINES	PR
46.	Pakistan Int'l Airlines	PAKISTAN	PK
47.	Polar Air Cargo Inc.	U.S.A.	PO
48.	Qantas Airways Ltd.	AUSTRALIA	QF
49.	Royal Nepal Airlines Corp.	NEPAL	RA
50.	Scandinavian Airlines System(Sas)	SWEDEN	SK
51.	Srilankan Airlines Ltd.	SRI LANKA	UL
52.	Singapore Airlines Ltd.	SINGAPORE	SQ
53.	Swiss Int'l Air Lines Ltd.	SWITZERLAND	LX
54.	Shanghai Airlines Co., Ltd.	CHINA	FM
55.	Thai Airways Int'l Public Co.,Ltd.	THAILAND	TG
56.	Turkish Airlines Inc.	TURKEY	TK
57.	United Airlines, Inc.	U.S.A.	UA
58.	Uzbekistan Airways	UZBEKISTAN	HY
59.	United Parcel	U.S.A.	5X
60.	Vietnam Airlines	VIETNAM	VN
61.	Virgin Atlantic	U.K.	VS

Conclusion

World geography studies the Traffic Conference, Time Differences, Longitude and Latitude, Greenwich Mean Time (GMT) and UTC, Calculation of Total Transportation Time, Airport 3-Letter codes, Airline 2 – letter codes relations between places, landscapes and people, describing travel and tourism as an economic, social and cultural activity. More concisely, it is all about the spatial and temporal dynamics, as well as the interactions between the tourism resources.

Chapter 3

Aircraft Familiarization

3.1 INTRODUCTION

An aircraft is a machine that is able to fly by gaining support from the air. It counters the force of gravity by using either static lift or by using the dynamic lift of an air foil, or in a few cases the downward thrust from jet engines. The human activity that surrounds aircraft is called aviation.

3.2 AIRCRAFT MANUFACTURERS

Everything about an aircraft manufacturing and assembly building must be driven by the manufacturing process, including process flow, process rate and process requirements. The building must fully support the process, in addition to "keeping the weather out." The manufacturing process must be well understood at a macro level by the facility planning and engineering team to ensure that an appropriate building concept Is developed that is integrated with manufacturing needs.

Manufacturing Process Type and Style

The manufacturing process type and style may include: flow line, fixed position assembly, parallel assembly, subassembly shops and fishbone assembly, all of which will determine the building's size and layout. Different manufacturing process flows will likely be used for different components or steps within the overall process.

Manufacturing Utilities

Most aircraft manufacturing has a high reliance on clean, dry compressed air as a primary utility. Therefore, providing redundancy, reliability, maintainability, and distribution and access flexibility for compressed air is critical. 400Hz aircraft power is often a critical test requirement. It needs to be close to the aircraft due to voltage loss. Also, exhaust air for fumes or heat processes is often necessary.

1. Airbus

Airbus is based in Europe with its headquarters in Toulouse, France and was established on December 18, 1970. In United States alone these are the following airlines that have an Airbus in their fleet: Allegiant Air, Frontier Airlines, Spirit, jetBlue, Delta Air Lines, United Airlines, US Airways and Virgin America. Not only airlines, but also cargo and express operators such as Federal Express and United Parcel Service had selected Airbus as their aircraft manufacturer. Revenue: 67 Billion USD (2014)

2. Boeing

The largest manufacturer of commercial jetliners and military aircraft combined. They also design and manufacture rotorcraft, electronic and defense systems, missiles, satellites, launch vehicles and advanced information and communication systems. Boeing is based in USA with its headquarters in Chicago, IL, United States and was established on July 15, 1916. We got to admit that Boeing is actually a leading aircraft manufacturer. Here is a list of their customers: Alaska Airlines, Air New Zealand, ANA All Nippon Airways, Cathay Pacific, Delta Air Lines,

Etihad Airways, Federal Express, Garuda Indonesia, Icelandair, KLM Royal Dutch Airlines and United Parcel Service. Revenue: 90.78 billion USD (2014)

3. Bombardier

The global transportation company which operates two kinds of businesses: Aerospace and Rail Transportation. In the Aerospace category, they are the world's third largest civil aircraft manufacturer. Bombardier is based in Canada with its headquarters in Dorval, Quebec and was established in 1942, present in over 60 countries on 5 continents. Here is some list of airlines that use Bombardier aircraft in their fleet: Lufthansa, Gulf Air, Odyssey Airlines, Korean Air, PrivatAir, Iraqi Airways, airBaltic and Swiss Global Air Lines as the most recent customer. The world's most comprehensive aircraft manufacturer's passion is to look far ahead and shape the future of mobility. Revenue: 10.5 billion USD (2014).

4. Embraer

The Brazilian rival of Bombardier, this is like the close competition between Airbus and Boeing. Embraer as mentioned is based in Brazil with its headquarters in São José dos Campos, São Paulo and was founded on August 19, 1969. Here is a list of airlines that use Embraer aircraft in their fleet: Air Canada, Alitalia, Flybe, Finnair, Kenya Airways, KLM, Saudi Arabian Airlines, Air Astana, Copa Airlines, Lufthansa, Virgin Australia and US Airways. With their E-jet products several countries were able to provide secondary markets that offer lower fares, which mean making a major contribution to travellers who can afford bigger aircraft for travel to still set foot on an aircraft. Revenue: 20.9 billion USD (2014).

5. Tupolev

When it comes to business either what sort, the Russian will always be part of the list since the Russians are known to be born competitive. Tupolev is a Russian aerospace and defense company which is headquartered in Moscow and was founded in 1922. If in case you are wondering what does Tupolev mean, it's actually the last name of the founder Andrei Nikolayevich Tupolev. Let me share with you a list of airlines that consist of Tupolev in their fleet: Air Koryo, Air Kyrgyzstan, Belavia and Kosmos Airlines. The capabilities of Tupolev don't only focus on airline travelling business development, but also overhaul for both civil and military aerospace products such as aircraft and weapons systems. It is also active with missile and naval aviation technologies. More than 18,000 Tupolev aircraft were produced for the USSR and the Eastern Bloc. Revenue: 55.982 million RUB (2014).

3.3 THE AIRCRAFT LAYOUT

Aircraft may be equipped with High frequency (HF) and Very high frequency (VHF) radios, direction finding equipment, Global Positioning System (GPS), instrument landing system (ILS) and Omni Directional Radio Range (VOR) Distance measuring equipment (DME) .

Aircraft-specific equipment should be listed in the aircraft publications under Special Equipment List (SEL).

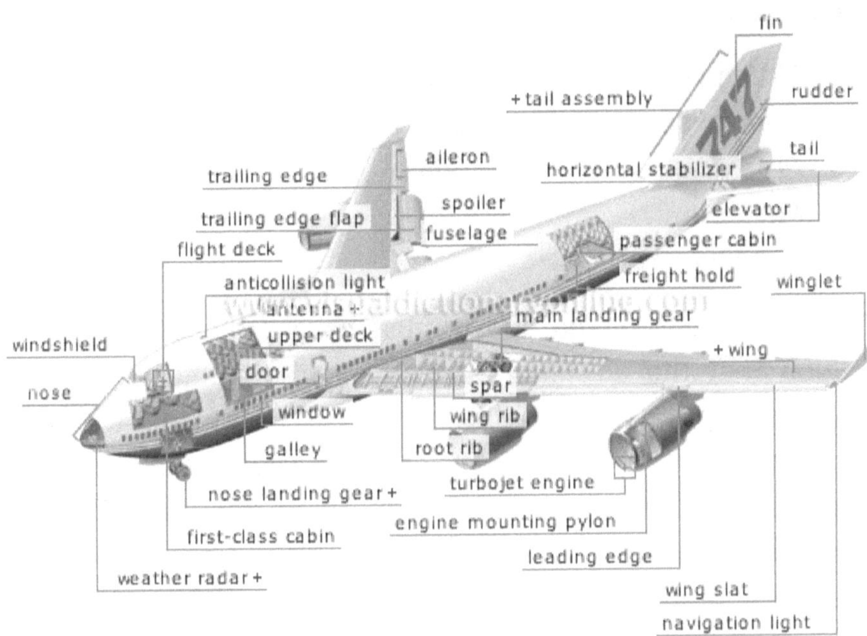

Figure 2: The Aircraft Layout
Source: www.visualdictionaryonline.com

Propeller pilot's fan, engine or cowling, wing, fuselage/ empennage, horizontal stabilizer, vertical stabilizer, landing gear, windows, fuel tanks etc. Control surfaces on next slides

Pilot controls: Yolk, rudder pedals, brakes, throttle, etc.

Three Axes: Longitudinal (roll – ailerons),

Lateral (pitch – elevator),

Vertical (yaw – rudder)

Basic components

There are different components all have to be completely integrated.

Configuration Concept:

- *Lifting surface arrangement*
- *Control surface(s) location*
- *Propulsion system selection*
- *Payload*
- *Landing Gear*

The components listed above must be coordinated in such a fashion that the airplane satisfies the requirements given in the following list. The configuration designer works to satisfy these requirements with input from the various team members. This is where the team member that dominates can distort the design in a way that keeps it from being the right response to the design requirements. To be successful the following criteria must be met.

Good Aircraft

- Aerodynamically efficient, including propulsion integration or streamlining
- Must balance near stability level for minimum drag
- Landing gear must be located relative to cg to allow rotation at take-off
- Adequate control authority must be available throughout the flight envelope
- Design to build easily and have low maintenance costs
- Today, commercial airplanes must be quiet and non-polluting

Systems

- Flight control system: Speed brake & vectoring nozzle(s)
- Fuel tank system coordinating with propulsion & structures
- Hydraulic and pneumatic

- Electrical system
- Landing gear system coordinating with configuration design
- Environmental control systems
- Avionics & sensor systems
- Anti-icing system(s)
- Defense/self – protection systems
- Weapon systems, if any coordinating with design
- Loading systems

3.4 IN FLIGHT SERVICE CLASSES

The aviation sector has become the most important segment in the economic development of a nation. It plays a vital role in moving people or products from one place to another, be it domestic or international, especially when the distances involved are far.

Airlines traditionally have three travel classes, *First Class*, *Business Class*, and *Economy Class.* Depending on the cabin configuration will determine how many classes of service are offered. Here's a breakdown of the classes of service:

- First Class, generally the most expensive and most comfortable accommodations available.
- Business Class, high quality, traditionally purchased by business travellers sometimes called executive class.
- Premium Economy, slightly better Economy Class seating greater distance between rows of seats; the seats themselves may or may not be wider than regular economy class.
- Economy Class also known as coach class or travel class, basic accommodation, commonly purchased by leisure travellers.

Airline Class of Service Codes

A – First Class Discounted

B – Economy/Coach – Usually an upgradable fare to Business

C – Business Class

D – Business Class Discounted

E – Shuttle Service (no reservation allowed) or Economy/Coach Discounted

F – First Class

G – Conditional Reservation

H – Economy/Coach Discounted – Usually an upgradable fare to Business

J – Business Class Premium

K – Economy/Coach Discounted

L – Economy/Coach Discounted

M – Economy/Coach Discounted – Usually an upgradable fare to Business

N – Economy/Coach Discounted

P – First Class Premium

Q – Economy/Coach Discounted

R – First Class Suite or Supersonic (discontinued)

S – Economy/Coach

T – Economy/Coach Discounted

U – Shuttle Service (no reservation needed/seat guaranteed)

V – Economy/Coach Discounted

W – Economy/Coach Premium

X – Economy/Coach Discounted

Y – Economy/Coach

Z – Business Class Discounted

3.5 CATERING LOADING

The flight catering industry is a very large, global activity. The total market size is estimated to be around 12 billion euros. More than 1 billion passengers are served each year. It is probably one of the most complex operational systems in the world.

For instance, a large-scale flight catering production unit may employ over 800 staff to produce as many as 25,000 meals per day during peak periods. Large international airlines may have more than 1,000 take-offs and landings every day. A single, long-haul Boeing 747 has over 40,000 items loaded on to it before it flies. All together these items weigh 6 metric tonnes and occupy a space of 60 cubic metres.

These items range from meals to toilet bags, from duty-free goods to first aid boxes, from newspapers to headsets. Food items must be fresh and items for personal passenger use must be clean and serviceable

These facts and others like them make flight catering unlike any other sector of the catering industry. While the way food is served on trays to airline passengers bears some resemblance to service styles in restaurants or cafeterias, the way food is prepared and cooked is increasingly resembling a food manufacturing plant. Certainly the hot kitchen in a typical production kitchen is often no more than 10% of the total floor area. The rest of the space is used for bonded stores, tray and trolley assembly, and flight wash-up. And almost certainly there are far more loaders and drivers employed than chefs. The way food and equipment is stored resembles a freight warehouse, and the way meals and equipment are transported and supplied has a close affinity to military-style logistics and distribution systems.

Prior to boarding, the catering truck arrives and load all the meal trays that are already set nicely inside the carts, and there are allocated carts specifically for beverages too. The galley person – who, by this time, has gotten the amount of the frozen meals for their galley as well as the manifest of passengers who requested special meals and will be seating in their area – checks the safety equipment in their respective station while the catering staff moving all the carts and the necessary stuff and put the oven racks with the frozen meals already stacked in into the ovens. The meals and the beverages loaded are usually for both outbound and inbound flight, the frozen meals for the inbound flight are kept in big boxes and stored, although some other airlines might reload the catering at their destination – it really depends on how the airline works it out.

Afterwards the galley person has to double check and count the meals both outbound and inbound meals, the beverages, and check for the necessary stuff: tea, coffee, sugar sachets, creamer sachets, extra cutlery sets, napkins, gloves, bread tongs, ice + ice buckets, plastic cups, paper cups, the lavatory supplies too, etc. They also have to make sure for any special meals to be in place i.e. the specific meals requested by passengers who will be sitting in their area, like vegetarian meals, halal meals, and/or baby meals. These passengers usually get their meals before other passengers, which is why if the passengers have requested for a specific meal in their booking, they're strongly encouraged not to switch their seat without advising the flight attendant.

The galley person then has to write down the exact amount of the meals and beverages and gives the list to the in-flight service manager every airline might have a different title for the person e.g. G2 or Grade 2. The service manager then fills in their catering form with the total numbers of everything and hands one copy to the purser and the other to the catering staff leader. Before take – off – usually during the briefing, the service manager informs the galley persons when to exactly turn the ovens on. Assuming that it's a 3 hour flight, the galley person's start heating up the meals 10-15 minutes before the seatbelt sign is turned off, although sometimes they might have to do it just slightly before reaching the cruising altitude to save up time and in case some ovens heat slower than others. While waiting for the meals to be ready, the galley person will start preparing the meal carts for each aisle and do other things like making pots of tea and coffee – other flight attendants might help but most galley persons prefer to do all these things themselves so they won't have to bump into other flight attendants while moving like an angry wasp in their galley.

When the meals are ready, the galley person transfers all the hot meals into the meal drawers and set them on top of the cart or inside – it depends on the airline's procedure. The galley person then calls the service manager and informs them that they're ready. Once the service manager gets the notification from all galleys, they give the galley person a thumb up to start serving in unison.

There are five major types of players in the airline catering business. These are the carriers (Airlines), the providers (Caterers), the suppliers (manufacturers), the distributors and the passengers. Each airline carrier decides what kind and how much food service they require and which flights need which types of service. Obviously food service can be used as a marketing tool; some airlines for instance, do not give as much service if they have no competition or if the flight is exceptionally short such as under 1 hour. Some passengers may be willing to forgo food on 'no frills' or 'peanuts' flights if fare prices are slashed. All of this is for the airline company to decide. The carrier must also decide whether to operate its own catering operation or which caterer to contract with. This decision is based upon location, availability, reliability, long time relationships, cost and convenience. Costs must be carefully negotiated by both the caterer and the carrier. The carrier cannot afford to pay too much as each fraction of a penny may add up to thousands of pounds, dollars etc., while the caterer cannot afford to accept too little as food prices may fluctuate or labour costs may increase, and the caterer must deliver a quality product to preserve not only their image but that of the airline. Manufacturers/suppliers who prepare food for the airlines also take advantage of economies of scale to purchase raw goods for the manufacture of airline meals, desserts, beverages and snacks. These suppliers can produce meals for economy class much more cheaply and efficiently than can most flight kitchens, hence catering companies tend to buy these meals from vendor/suppliers.

3.5.1 Role of Food on Board

How important are food and on board service to the airlines? Some airlines use food as a marketing tool. A number of airlines advertise their product by making food the focal point. But food as a marketing tool has only a limited impact. Surveys over a number of years suggest that passengers appear most concerned about safety, on time performance, scheduling/ticketing issues, the aircraft's physical surroundings such as seat and leg comfort, and gate check-in and boarding.

3.5.2 Flight Catering Logistics

Logistics is concerned with adding value and reducing waste across the whole flight catering system. It is particularly concerned with non-consumable or non-disposable stock items such as crockery, glassware, trays, etc., although increasingly it is addressing other types of inventory too (particularly alcoholic beverages and duty free items). In order to use these stocks effectively and efficiently, logistics is concerned with:

- Material demand forecasting
- Equipment sector or shelf life
- Sourcing of products
- Contracting suppliers
- Managing purchase contracts
- Transportation of stocks
- warehousing of stocks
- Inventory management of stocks and 'dwell time' (time not in use)
- Stock balancing across the network
- Galley and trolley planning

3.5.3 Airline Caterer Contracts

One expert (McCool, 1996) has described the relationship between airlines and caterers: "It is somewhat like soliciting guests to stay at a hotel property.

Flight Catering and then, once solicited, having the guests specify the type and brand of amenities, linens and furnishings that will be in their rooms when they arrive; having the guests sometimes bring their own supply of amenities, food and beverages with them and having property secure them in safe storage and issue them on guests' request; having the guests regularly conduct quality control surveys of the property; and finally having the guest have a say in determining what rates they are going to pay for their stay." In view of this complex relationship there needs to be clarity about the nature of the contract between the two parties, and in a form that is legally binding. The relationship between an airline and caterer is based on service delivery. The airline requires its catering supplier to deliver on certain key variables, such as:

- Consistency of food product
- Accuracy of uplift
- On time delivery
- Value for money
- Service relationships
- Health, hygiene and safety
- Innovation
- Overall operational performance

3.5.4 Role of Airlines

As has been suggested, the flight caterer's customer is not the fare-paying passenger but actually the airline. The caterer must respond to the demands and wishes of the airline and any wider motives that the airline may be seeking to develop. The airline though, theoretically at least, seeks to establish what the 'flying customer' might require, and attempts, through the caterer, to interpret and respond to those wishes. Within the airline, individual groups of people will, in turn, be customers. The cabin staff who serve the meals face a dichotomy. They often had had no input into the planning or preparation of the meals concerned, but are yet customers of the catering providers. They offer and serve a product of which they have limited knowledge to a further customer. In one study, many cabin crew believed that decisions on the number of meals and the content of menus are made by the caterers, whereas in practice these decisions were made by the airline management (Pedrick et al., 1993).

3.5.5 Role of Suppliers

Suppliers may supply either caterers or airlines, increasingly the latter. If, the supplier receives direct orders from the airlines, they deliver their goods to flight production units, which may be operated by contracted caterers. Airlines buy direct from suppliers for a number of reasons:

- Continuity of supply in all their stations
- To negotiate a discount
- To link to the brand image of the product
- Readiness's of the supplier to provide products that meet the contract specification Likewise, suppliers have two approaches to manufacturing their products. Some supply airlines or caterers with their standard products, whereas others make and supply specialist products specifically designed for the flight industry.

For each of the stages in the flight catering operation, there are some features that are unique to flight catering. These derive from one simple fact: while the food is prepared on the ground it will be consumed in the air. *This impacts on:*

- *Customers and their needs* the prime motivation for travel is not eating
- *Menus* some food and drink items are not suitable for consumption in pressurised cabins 10 km above the ground
- *Production methods* the volume of business necessitates large-scale meal production

- *Service style* since passengers are seated in rows of aircraft seats, tray service predominates
- *Shelf-life* the time difference between production on the ground and consumption in the air which determines the adoption of cook–chill methodologies
- *Transportation* moving trayed meals from production unit to aircraft and then storing on board is based around modular trolleys

These challenges have always existed since the earliest days of commercial passenger air travel. Introduction to flight catering of ideas very early in its development which are still in use today the aircraft galley (1920), the in-flight movie (1929), male and female cabin crew (1930), the flight production unit (1938), on-board ovens (1946), and so on. Having looked at the history and development of flight catering, this book will now examine in detail every aspect of the industry. Appropriately, it will end with a chapter that looks at innovation in the industry what might happen in the industry in the future.

3.6 UNIT LOADING DEVICES (ULD)

i) Introduction

The term Unit Load Device (ULD) means any type of container with an integral pallet, or aircraft pallet whether or not owned by an IATA member, and whether or not considered to be aircraft equipped.

Cargo is the source of revenue for freight operations and can also be a significant portion of passenger airline revenue. On passenger aircraft, cargo is carried in the lower hold. On freighters, cargo is also carried on the main deck. In large

Boeing aircraft, cargo is loaded and carried in various pallets and containers, known as Unit Load Devices (ULD).

ii) Definition

Unit load devices is a unit in which dead load is bulk and subsequently loaded as a unit into the aircraft.

iii) Background

The use of unit load devices ULDs will facilitate the processing of large quantities of baggage/cargo/mail within relatively short ground time.

Loading and unloading of such quantities as single items would require significantly more time resulting in extended aircraft ground times. The main deck of freighter aircraft and in some cases the lower compartments are equipped with on board systems designed to position and restrain unit load devices.

iv) Purpose

The purpose of wide body aircraft brought the idea of unitized loading Unloading in the aviation industry. Under this system the dead load baggage, mail and cargo is loaded first in an empty unit load device and then this loaded ULD is put inside the aircraft cargo compartment as one piece and is guarded at its place by locks on the floor panel.

This procedure helped the airlines:

a. In minimizing the time consumed in loading and unloading of bulk load.
b. In curtailing the ground time of wide body aircraft
c. In guaranteeing the safety of load
d. In curbing the high rate of damages, thefts and pilferages

e. In reducing the accidents and incidents faced during bulk loading and unloading of dead load.

f. In making maximum utilization of inside space killed by the aircraft contour

g. In marketing the complete ULD space under Bulk Utilization Program (BUP)

h. In improving the standard of services and ground handling.

i. In planning pre-flight loads and functions

j. In accepting last minute loads without involving lot of time causing unnecessary delays

k. In carrying the load from origin to destination without the need for reloading the cargo into different units at interim or transit points

A Unit Load Device is thus a container or pallet made of light and strong metal suitable for loading prescribed tonnage of load, and easily loadable inside the aircraft compartment at allocated places, where these units are secured with the help of locks system on the floor panel. These ULDs loaded on aircraft and secured with the help of locks become an integral part of the aircraft.

TYPES OF ULDs

- Containers
- Pallets, Nets
- Igloos.

1. Containers

Containers are regarded as small aircraft holds in themselves, which can be removed from the aircraft and loaded/unloaded at the passenger or warehouse area. Like conventional holds, containers have certain structural limits that must not be exceeded, unless the correct procedures are followed. Container requires proper underneath support and the same standards as under should be used. Maximum gross weight per container is inscribed on the container marking plate. This must not be exceeded and the maximum shell weight limit should also be observed. Maximum loading densities for the floor must not be exceeded.

a) Certified Containers:

These are strong enough in themselves to restrain the load they carry and protect the aircraft from damage. The hold walls and ceilings of the aircraft do not have to be very strong because the containers do the work, this may make the aircraft structure unsuitable for bulk loading or carriage of Non Certified Containers.

b) Non-Certified Containers:

These are convenient containers or "Over Packs" used for the ease of loading and the protection of cargo. They are not strong enough to retain loads during any violent in-flight conditions and may only be loaded on aircraft with holds that are certified as having walls and ceilings that permit bulk loading.

2. Pallets

platform with a flat under-surface to standard aircraft requirements on which goods are assembled and secured by net/straps/igloos,and subsequently lock into the aircraft, to achieve rapid loading/unloading on compatible aircraft conveying and restraint systems. As such, it becomes a component of the aircraft loading and restraint system. Loaded pallets must always be fully supported from underneath with roller section, ball mats or inverted casters.

Pallets are certified units that can be regarded as sections of the aircraft floor, which can be removed from the aircraft to ease the loading and unloading. Like the aircraft floor, pallets have certain structural limits that must not be exceeded.

Pallets normally arrive at the aircraft side with the load restraint by a certified net.

NETS:

A network of webbing affixed to an aircraft within its holds or to an aircraft ULD for the purpose of restraining a load within the hold or in the ULD. The net is an integral part of the aircraft restraint system, the pallet and net(s) are approved by the airworthiness authority as one unit, therefore only those nets approved with specified pallets shell be used together.

3. Igloo "NON STRUCTURAL IGLOO"

A bottomless rigid shell made of fiberglass, metal or other suitable material. Its shape conforms to the contours of cargo aircraft envelopes. It covers the maximum usable area of an aircraft pallet to which it is secured during flight. This shell used in combination with an aircraft pallet and net assembly is known as a non-structural igloo. Igloos are intended to protect the interior of aircraft from damage and to provide a framework container into which cargo can be loaded. When not in use they should be kept on a pallet on a properly supported surface. A net must always be used to secure a structural igloo to the pallet. The contents in the igloo shall be properly secured to prevent load shifting High density items should be individually secured with tie-downs, stowage or donnage. The igloo shell is not subject to airworthiness requirements as it is always used in conjunction with an aircraft pallet and net, the shell, however, is to be examined for cracks, holes and damaged hardware.

Handling of ULDS

ULDs are expensive equipment and should be handled in a proper manner. The loading and handling of ULDs should be carried out with extreme care to ensure in-flight safety, reliability and maximize equipment life.

- ULDS must be base supported all the times to prevent damage to under surface.
- No loads to be placed on roof of the containers.
- Do not load containers in the aircraft unless doors are properly closed.
- Never cut nets or straps to release net.
- ULDS are not to be lifted directly by forklifts.
- ULDs empty or loaded must not be dropped from the dollies onto the floor.
- ULDs empty or loaded must not be dragged along the ground.
- Do not tip containers on their sides or ends.
- Ensure transfer levels are made when transferring ULDs.

Loading of ULDs and Serviceability Check:

For reasons of safety the use of defective ULDs is prohibited. Ensure that the

ULDs are serviceable prior to loading. Defective ULDs must be reported to the airlines concerned in order to arrange dispatch to their repair centre.

a) Pallets:

The pallet is to be examined for gouges, depressions, delaminated or dented panels, cracked edge rails, or missing corner or rivets. Edge rails are not acceptable if there are any cracks, missing corners, or missing/broken net attachment points.

An unladed pallet sitting on a flat surface shall not bow to the extent that the edge rail bottom corner would be more than 50mm (2 in) above the surface. The top surface of a pallet edge rail shall not be more than 3 cm above the conveying surface when in a loaded condition. There shall be no missing, cracked, worn or otherwise damaged restraint or handling provisions.

b) NETS:

The net assembly is to be examined for frayed or damaged netting and missing or damaged hardware. Frayed netting shall not be such as to reduce the strength by more than 10%.

There shall not be any broken, cut or otherwise parted straps. There shall not be any broken, deformed or crushed to the point of non-functioning, or missing strap adjustment hardware, buckles or pallet attachment fittings

Correct ULD loading procedures:

- Correct shape and height ensure by using contour frame.
- Load big and heavy pieces on the ULD base.
- Load small and light packages at the top of the heavy pieces.
- Whenever possible, interlock layers of cargo.
- Heavy items should be loaded on spreader boards and lashed down as per lashing procedures.
- Packages on open pallets should be stacked so that the load is stable and will not fall sideways.
- Pack items tightly together leaving as few gaps and spaces as possible.
- Ensure the aircraft hold contour is not exceeded.

Aircraft Loading

1. Principle of Loading:

Following are the principles of Loading:

- I)   Load from forward and offload from rear hold.
- II)   First on Last off and Last on First off.
- III)   Spread load evenly in forward and aft hold.
- IV)   Do not block baggage by cargo and mail.

2. Loading Regulations:

- Staff responsible for aircraft loading and other associated activities must be conversant with the laid down regulations and procedures.
- Utmost care must be exercised during loading operations to avoid damage to the aircraft frame, floors, doors, doorsills, locks and unit load devices.
- Aircraft compartments, containers and vehicles are to be thoroughly checked after unloading to ensure that no items have been overlooked.
- Loading instruction is to be strictly followed while loading/ unloading the aircraft compartments.
- Always offload baggage first and send it to the terminal building as quickly as possible.
- Ensure all goods are adequately and correctly labeled to destination.
- Checking of cargo and mail against relevant documents is to be absolutely correct.
- Goods, inadequately packed must be repacked before loading.
- Instructions for loading of special items must be rigidly followed.

- Place heavier items at the bottom.
- Stack neatly for maximum stability and maximum use of available volume.
- Do not exceed the published floor limitations. Whenever necessary, use spreader to spread the load.
- Separation is to be maintained between incompatible dangerous goods as per dangerous goods regulations.
- All ULDs should be inspected prior to loading to ensure that no broken edges or damaged exist which may damage goods and aircraft holds.
- The loads must be secured in accordance with airline's regulations.
- Articles likely to cause damage to other loads or to the aircraft must be secured individually.
- Ensure that the separation nets are properly secured to subdivide cargo holds/compartments.
- After loading is over, ensure that the door protector nets are installed, doors are closed and properly secured.

Unit Load Devices – ULD Procedures

To obtain the weight and the center of gravity of an aircraft, among other items the real weight of cargo and/or mail load shall be determined.

Responsibility for the application of correct cargo and mail weights in the weight and balance calculation and documentation remains entirely with LTU department in charge of aircraft handling and/or its agents and contractors at other stations.

ULD Tags

After completion of loading and weighing of pallets and/or containers, an ULD tag shall be completed for each individual

ULD. The reverse side of the container/pallet cargo ULD tag is intended or may be used for empty ULD's.

Aircraft ULDs

These are units that interface directly with an Aircraft loading and restraint system. They meet all normal restraint requirements without the use of supplementary equipment – providing they are loaded in accordance with the specific Aircraft Load and Balance Manual. Such units become an integral part of the Aircraft structure, when loaded and are typically Certified Aircraft Containers or Pallet and Net assemblies. Note: The Aircraft Load and Balance Manual includes controls for-

- The type, number and positions, that ULDs can be loaded.
- Their allowable Max Gross Weights
- Acceptable alternate ULD loading arrangements such as: – Carriage of loads exceeding normal allowances. Load limitations with broken/missing restraint components. These controls may effect direct interlining of ULDs between Aircraft Types. Aircraft ULDs may be loaned to shippers and agents for loading purposes provided they can prove that they are equipped and capable to handle them in accordance with the Aircraft Load and Balance Manual(s).

Non-Aircraft ULDs

These units do not interface with the aircraft restraint system. They must be registered with IATA and conform to IATA standard specifications. Non-aircraft ULDs, in order to be eligible for rating incentives, must be owned by a shipper or agent. With around 900,000 aircraft ULDs in service representing a replacement value of over USD $1 Billion, ULDs are expensive assets that require correct handling. Many people in the industry do not know that ULDs are aircraft parts and directly contribute to flight safety. Dangerous Goods, Live Animals and Human Remains will not be accepted in a ULD, either rated under methods A or B. Further information on the rules applicable to ULDs and full rating tables can be obtained from: The Air Cargo Tariff (TACT).

3.7 BULK LOADING LIMITATIONS

bulk carrier means any of the following ships which is of 500 gross tonnage or more: a ship constructed with a single deck, top-side tanks and hopper-side tanks in cargo spaces and intended primarily to carry dry cargo in bulk; or an ore carrier, where "ore carrier" means a sea-going single deck ship having two longitudinal bulkheads and a double bottom throughout the cargo region and intended for the carriage of ore cargoes in the centre holds only ; or a combination carrier means a tanker designed to carry oil or alternatively solid bulk cargo.

"Dry cargo in bulk" or "solid bulk cargo"

Dry cargo in bulk means any material other than liquid or gas, consisting of a combination of particles, granules or any other large pieces of material generally uniform in composition, which is loaded directly into the cargo spaces of a ship without intermediate form of containment. excluding grain; bulk cargoes are cargoes that are transported en masse, in large volumes in specially constructed ships.

The cargo may be in the following modes:

    a.   Dry
    b.   Liquid or
    c.   Gas

i) Types of bulk cargoes

Bulk cargo can be classified into:

- Liquid bulk cargo – includes crude oil, refined oil products, liquefied petroleum gases and cooking oil transported in bulk ships and oil tankers
- Discharged in specialized oil terminals e.g. Kipevu oil terminal (KOT) for crude oil, and Shimanzi oil terminal (SOT) for refined oil products in Mombasa port
- Most are of dangerous nature and require specialized handling Dry bulk cargo – include edible foods such as maize, beans, wheat; raw materials as clinker, iron ore bauxite and soda ash
- It also includes industrial and agricultural products as fertilizers, cement etc
- Conveyance of such cargo is done using specially built ship with very wide hatch opening sand sophisticated tank arrangements to ensure stability

ii) Methods of handling bulk cargo

- Different methods are used to handle different types of bulk cargo.
- Some dry bulk cargo handling facilities available at the port of include Bamburi cement, Magadi soda, Grain handling (Grain bulk Ltd) Bulk cargo can be handled using different methods namely:
- Grabs
- Magnetic grabs
- Conveyor belt
- Evacuators

Requirements in relation to the operational suitability of bulk carriers for loading and unloading solid bulk cargoes

Terminal operators shall satisfy themselves as to the operational suitability of bulk carriers for the loading or unloading of solid bulk cargoes by checking that the bulk carriers comply with the following requirements:

1. They shall be provided with cargo holds and hatch openings of sufficient size and such a design to enable the solid bulk cargo to be loaded, stowed, trimmed and unloaded satisfactorily;
2. They shall be provided with the cargo hold hatch identification numbers as used in the loading or unloading plan. The location, size and colour of these numbers shall be clearly visible to and identifiable by the operator of the terminal loading or unloading equipment;
3. Their cargo hold hatches, hatch operating systems and safety devices shall be in good functional order and used only for their intended purpose;
4. List indicating lights, if fitted, shall be tested prior to loading or unloading and proved to be operational;
5. If required to have an approved loading instrument on board, this instrument shall be certified and operational to carry out stress calculations during loading or unloading;
6. Propulsion and auxiliary machinery shall be in good functional order;
7. Deck equipment related to mooring and berthing operations shall be operable and in good order and condition.

Example of Load Securing A320 (bulk loaded)

The divider and door net in each compartment must be closed at any time. Additional tie-down is normally not required except for individual items of load which by their nature, shape or density may constitute a hazard. They must be restrained, which can be achieved by filling the cargo hold or net section volumetrically, or by tie-down. When filled up to ¾ of height, the cargo hold or net section is considered to be volumetrically full.

Packages weighing more than 150kg shall be restraint or individually tied-down. Single packages should be tied-down. Tie-down of loads to aircraft structure is achieved by straps or nets connected to the tie down points located on the cargo hold floor. Each tie-down point is designed to an ultimate load of 906kg, in any direction.

Conclusion

The efficient operation of the air transport industry depends on fast and accurate services, the in-flight service manager is chosen by seniority years of flight experience and they're in charge for all the meal service in the flight so they have to get the exact amount of meals and beverages from each galley. Terminal operators must follow the requirements in relation to the operational suitability of bulk carriers for loading and unloading solid bulk cargoes.

Chapter 4

The Air Cargo Agency and Acceptance

4.1 INTRODUCTION

IATA Cargo Agents should ensure that the security standards described in the Recommended Practice are followed. In increased threat situations, supplementary security measures may be required by air carriers or appropriate authorities. The Cargo Agency Conference Resolutions, which embody the rules for accreditation of cargo agents, include text specifically relating to security. This requires the agent to implement security controls as required by the appropriate authorities and which may be supplemented by Member air carriers. Cargo agents' security procedures should embody those in this Recommended

Practice and include the following recommended provisions:

1. Security requirements for the packing, storage, transportation and delivery of consignments to an approved agent or carrier;
2. Established procedures for the identification and verification of persons including: Account Consignors, Known Consignors or Regulated Agents and the recording of their details;
3. Requirements for the physical protection and safe-keeping of consignments held in their custody prior to delivery to the carrier;

4. Criteria for the training and recurrent training of agents' staff involved with security screening, storage, transportation and delivery of consignments.

Air Cargo Guide The official scheduling guide for scheduled air freight services, published by the Official Airline, Guides (OAG). It contains current Domestic and international cargo flight schedules, including freighter, wide body and combination passenger-cargo flights. Each monthly issue also contains information on air carriers' special services, airline and aircraft decoding, airport codes, air carrier and freight forwarders directory, customs information, glossary of ULD terms and information, cargo charter airlines, interline air freight agreements, aircraft loading charts and more.

Air Cargo, Inc (ACI)

A ground Service Corporation jointly owned by several U.S. scheduled airlines. In addition to its airline owners, ACI serves over 50 air freight forwarders and international air carriers as associate participants. One of ACI's major functions is to facilitate the surface movement of air freight by negotiating and supervising the performance of a nationwide series of contracts under which trucking companies provide both local pickup and delivery service at airport cities and over-the-road truck service to move air freight to and from points not directly served by the airlines. ACI publishes a directory of these trucking services, listing points served in the United States and the applicable pickup and delivery rates. Other services include claims inspection, terminal handling, and telemarketing service, group purchasing equipment, supplies, insurance and Electronic Data Interchange (EDI) services.

Air Express Shipments for which the airline provides a guaranteed level of expedited service, such as overnight, at a premium charge. It may be restricted as to package weight and size. Air Freight Property other than mail Express, or passenger baggage tendered to an airline for transportation.

Air Freight Forwarder

A Service organization which serves the dual role of air carrier usually indirect and shipper, to the shipper the air freight forwarder is an indirect air carrier because it receives freight under its own tariff, yet does not actually operate the airplanes. The air freight forwarder provides pick-up and delivery service to and from the shippers dock, consolidates shipments into larger units, prepares shipping documentation and tenders shipments to the airlines. To the airlines, the air freight forwarder is a shipper. Ordinarily an air freight forwarder is classed as an indirect air carrier; however, some air freight forwarders operate their own aircraft.

Airline Tariff Publishing Co. (ATPCO) Publisher of airline industry tariffs setting forth rates and rules applicable to air freight. Tariffs are available on a subscription basis. Airport Mail Facility (AMF) a U.S. Postal Service facility located on or adjacent to an airport that is primarily engaged in the dispatch, receipt, and transfer of mail directly with air carriers.

Air Transport Association of America (ATA) a trade and service organization for U.S. scheduled airlines. In the cargo field, ATA works with the airlines, the Government, and shippers in developing improved standards and techniques in all phases of air cargo. ATA is an authoritative source of information on cargo matters such as air freight packaging practices, automation, data on air freight growth and statistical data on air cargo services.

Air Waybill (Airbill)

A shipping document used by the airlines for air freight. It serves as a contract for carriage and includes carrier conditions of carriage such as limits of liability and claims procedures. The air waybill also contains shipping instructions to the airline, a description of the commodity, and applicable transportation charges.

The airline industry has adopted a standard formatted air waybill that accommodates both domestic and international traffic.

Allowable Cabin Load (ACL)

The maximum payload weight that can be carried on an airplane on a specific route segment under a specific set of operation conditions

Articles of Extraordinary Value (A.E.V.) Commodities identified as high value items.

Automatic Proof of Delivery (P.O.D.) Information automatically sent to payer containing name of person who signed for the package with date and time of delivery.

Baggage

Passenger personal property or other passenger articles transported in connection with a journey. Unless otherwise specified, it includes both checked and unchecked baggage.

Baggage Cart

A towed vehicles used for ramp transport of bulk freight, baggage, and mail

Belly, Pits or Holds Compartments located beneath the cabin of an aircraft and used for the carriage of cargo and passenger baggage.

Belt Loader

A vehicle equipped with an adjustable height belt conveyor designed for loading/unloading bulk cargo.

Bill of Lading

A document by which a carrier receipts for goods and contracts to move them in air freight, the air waybill serves as the bill of lading and is the contract for carriage.

Break Bulk Disassembling or unpacking a consolidated shipment for delivery or for consignment

Bulk Cargo Loose cargo, not unitized, not loaded in containers or on pallets.

Bulk Cargo Carts Mobile units which transfer the bulk cargo from the airplane to the cargo handling terminal or to other airport locations

Bulk Loaded Cargo loaded as loose pieces into airplane compartments.

Cargo Aircraft

Aircraft for the carriage of cargo only, rather than the combination of passengers and cargo, Cargo aircraft carry palletized or containerized traffic on the main deck and either unitized or bulk cargo on the lower deck. Cargo aircraft are normally equipped with special cargo loading systems on the main deck. Also referred to as freighters or all-cargo aircraft

Cargo Agent: An agent appointed by an airline to solicit and process international air freight for shipments. Cargo agents are paid commissions by the airline.

Cargo Loader: Mobile equipment with elevation platforms and powered rollers for loading/unloading ULDs on airplane main decks or lower lobes. It may be "scissor" or "post" design, or a forklift equipped with a non – powered roller platform. Cartage Agent Ground service operator who provides pickup and delivery in areas not served directly by air carrier.

Chargeable Weight

The weight of the shipment used in determining air freight charges. The chargeable weight may be the dimensional weight or the actual scale weight of the shipment. See dimensional weight.

Charges Collect Transportation charges may include pickup and/or delivery and are entered on the air waybill to be collected from the consigned. Equivalent terms are "freight collect" or "charges forward."

Charter Service

The temporary hiring of an aircraft, usually on a trip basis, for the movement of cargo or passengers

Check Digit Number

A single digit of the air waybill number used to insure that the air waybill number is correctly entered into a computer system.

Collect Charges

The transportation practice under which the receiver of the goods pays charges

Collect on Delivery (COD)

A transportation service under which the purchase price of the goods in collected by the carrier from the receiver at the time of delivery, Payment Is subsequently transmitted to the shipper. Carriers charge a nominal fee for this service. Payment is due upon delivery. There are no credit provisions in COD service.

COMAT

An acronym for "company-owned material", The airlines own property such as Spare parts, station supplies, ticket stock, etc. carried on the airlines own airplanes.

Combi Airplane An airplane configured to carry both passengers and unitized cargo on the main deck.

Combination Carriers Scheduled air carriers who transport both passengers and cargo in passenger configured aircraft, with cargo restricted to the lower deck compartments.

Consignee

The person or firm whose name appears on the air waybill as the party to whom the goods are to be delivered by the carrier

Consignment Synonym for shipment

A shipment of one or more pieces of property, accepted by the carrier from one shipper at one time, receipted for in one lot, and moving on one air waybill.

Consignor

The person or firm whose name appears on the air waybill as the party contracting with the carrier for carriage of the goods, usually the shipper

Consolidation

A number of separate shipments that have been assembled into one shipment for movement on one air waybill from one location to another

Consolidator

An entity that provides consolidation services, joining multiple shipments into a single shipment from tender to an air carrier, An Air Freight Forwarder performs the function of a consolidator.

Container

A unit load device (ULD) which interfaces directly with the airplane cargo handling and restraint system.

Containerization

The practice or technique of using a boxlike device (containers) in which a number of packages are stored, protected, and handled as a single unit in transit. Container, Non-structural A bottomless, rigid shell made of fiberglass, metal or other suitable material used in combination with an airplane pallet and net assembly.

Container Rate

A rate for the transportation of an entire container or unit of Load (ULD) at a uniform charge, regardless of the weight of its content, unless a pivot weight is specified Container, Structural A rigid structure that performs the function of a ULD without the use of restraining net.

Contoured ULD

A ULD shaped to fit the airplane envelope to utilize the maximum space available.

Contract Rate

An unpublished rate established by contractual agreement between a carrier and a regular shipper, usually linked to a minimum volume requirement over a specified time period. Contract rates are sometimes a specified percentage discount of published rates.

Convertible Airplane

An airplane which can be converted from an all-passenger configuration to an all-cargo configuration or vice-versa, or to various configurations of passengers and cargo.

Coordinated movement

The coordination and preplanning of schedules and air transport services between two or more carriers or shippers, often involving interline agreements and joint rates. Such services may involve the use of all forms of air as well as surface transport. Courier Attendant who accompanies cargo shipment(s) Also attendant such as groom or veterinarian who accompany rare horses or other live animals

Cube Rule

A tariff basis stating the minimum density on which weight-based charges are to be computer

Cubic Capacity

The carrying capacity within an aircraft or container, expressed either in cubic feet, cubic inches, cubic centimeters or cubic meters.

Customhouse Broker

A broker who is certified by the U.S. Bureau of Customs to act for importers and other businessmen in handling the sequence of Customs formalities and other details related to the legal importation of goods.

Customs

The designated government authority that regulates the flow of goods to/from a country and collects duties levied by a country on imports and exports, the term also applies to the procedures involved in such collection.

Declared Value for Carriage

The value of goods declared to the carrier by the shipper for the purposes of determining charges of or establishing the limit of the carrier's liability for loss, damage, or delay. See Valuation Charges.

Declared Value for Customs

The selling price of the contents or the replacement cost if the contents are not for resale. The amount mush is equal to or greater than the declared value.

Deferred

Air Freight Property received for air transportation at a level of service lower than standard service e.g., space available and transported at a lower charge than standard air freight.

Deferred Rate

A rate that is lower than the corresponding standard rates for a comparable shipment. A shipper using a deferred rate agrees to accept a lower level or service in return for the lower rate.

Demurrage

The detention of containers by shippers or receives of freight beyond a specified grace period. The airlines tender carrier owned containers to the customer for loading and unloading of the unit. In the event the container is not returned to the carrier within a specified time usually 36-48 hours a charge may be assessed by the carrier for each 24-hour period or fraction there of beyond the allowed time.

Density

Density is weight per unit of volume. Density is computed by dividing a shipments weight by its cubic volume.

Department of Transportation (DOT)

An executive department of the U.S. Government established by the Department of Transportation Act of 1966 for the purposes of developing national transportation policies. As a result of the Airline Deregulation Act of 1978, the Dot acquired many of the functions of the CAB.

Dimensional Weight or Volume Weight

A computed weight based on a minimum density requirement. It is used to determine the freight charges for low dense shipments. It is computed by dividing the shipment volume by the minimum density requirement. The Dimensional Weight Rule was developed to insure fair compensation for low – density shipments. When a given shipment falls below the minimum density requirement, dimensional weight rather than actual weight is used to calculate the transportation charged. Minimum density requirements vary from carrier to carrier. Some carriers give discounts for shipments of high-density goods.

Direct Air Carrier

An air carrier that operates airplanes on a scheduled or contract (charter) basis, or both, and provides transportation for a charge, an airline as opposed to a freight forwarder

Dolly

A piece of equipment used to move containers or pallets around the airport with the aid of a tractor.

Duty

The Tax imposed on imports by the Customs authority of a country. Duties are generally based on the value of the goods (ad valorem duties), but may be based on weight or quantity, specific duties, or a combination of value and other factors or compound duties.

Electronic Data Interchange (EDI)

A computerized system for communicating information about a shipment, including tracking and tracing, air waybill information and customs documentation

Embargo

Temporary refusal to accept traffic for transportation at certain points or in certain routes due to emergencies, limitation of facilities, or other abnormal circumstances

Exception Ratings Rates set at a certain percentage above the general commodity rates because they apply to commodities that require special handling, such as live animals, human remains, or automotive vehicles.

Export License

A Government document which permits the "Licensee" to engage in the export of designated goods to certain destinations.

Express Small parcel shipments for which premium usually overnight service is provided. External Dimensions, ULD the Extreme outside measurement, including any handles or other protrusions, ULD the amount of space a ULD occupies in an airplane, calculated using the extreme external dimensions of the unit.

Federal Aviation Administration (FAA)

Created under the Federal Aviation Act of 1958 as the Federal Aviation Agency and charged with the responsibility of promulgation operational standards and procedures for all classes of aviation in the United States. With the creation of the cabinet level Department of Transportation in 1966 FAA became a unit within the new Department and received the new designation Federal Aviation Administration. The FAA Administrator, however, continues to be a presidential appointee and the FAA remains a separate entity with most of its former functions. In the field of air cargo FAA promulgates certain stress standards, which must be me in the tie down of cargo in flight.

Foreign Trade Zone

A port designated by the Government of a country for duty-free entry of any non-prohibited goods. Merchandise may be stored, displayed, used for manufacturing, etc. within the zone and re-exported without duties being paid. Duties are imposed on the merchandise or items manufactured from the merchandise only when the goods pass from the foreign trade zone into an area of the country subject to the Customs authority. Free Along Side (FAS) a basis of pricing meaning the price of goods alongside a transport vessel at a specified location. The buyer is responsible for loading the goods onto the transport vessel and pays all the cost of shipping beyond that location.

Free Domicile

A term used in international transportation where the shipper pays all transportation charges and any applicable duties and/or taxes.

Free On Board (FOB)

A pricing term indication that the quoted price includes the cost of loading the goods into transport vessels at the specified place

Freight

Generally refers to air cargo, but does include air express, mail or passenger baggage.

General Commodity Rate (GCR)

An air freight rate applicable to all commodities except those for which specific rates have been filed such rates are based on weight and distance and are published for each pair of cities an airline serves.

General Order (GO)

Merchandise not entered within 5 working days after arrival of the carrier and subsequently stored at the risk and expense of the importer.

Gross Weight Entire weight of a shipment including the weight of containers or tare weight and packaging material, on an air waybill, the tare weight when applicable and shipment weight are listed separately.

Hazardous materials (Hazmat) Items of freight that is inherently harmful and classified under Title 49, Code of Federal Regulations (CFR). Hazardous Materials may only be transported under certain conditions relative to packaging, quantity carried, airplane type, location on board the airplane, etc., and in conformance with applicable rules.

High Capacity Airplane Equivalent to wide-bodied airplanes. Specifically refers to B747, B767, B777, A300, A330, A340, DC10, MD-11, L-1011, IL-86 & IL-96.

Hold For Pickup Freight to be held at the carrier's destination location for pickup by the recipient.

Hub and Spoke System

An airline route pattern that directs traffic from many cities into a central hub designed to connect with other flights to final destinations. They system maximizes fleet utilization by connecting many markets through a central hub with fewer flights than would be required to connect each pair of cities in a point to point system.

Igloo

A structural or non-structural container

Import License

A document required and issued by some national governments authorizing the importation of goods into their individual counties.

Indirect Air Carrier

Indirect air carriers are those businesses authorized to receive freight from shippers under their own tariff, but who utilize certified air carriers, direct air carriers, to perform the air transportation services.

Integrated Carrier

A carrier that provides door-to-door air cargo transportation using its own or contracted airplanes and motor trucks, and performs this service under the authority of a single air waybill e.g. United Parcel Service and Federal Express.

Intermodal Compatibility

The capability to transfer a shipment from one mode of transport to another, as from airplane to highway truck, to railway freight car, to ocean vessel, certain aircraft can accommodate large types of standard containers commonly used in surface transport.

Intermodal Container

A structural container designed for carriage on airplanes, trucks, rail cars, and ocean vessels and equipped with corner fittings for restraint on a truck chassis and/or for lifting by crane or other loading mechanism.

Internal Fittings A means of securing cargo inside a container

Internal Volume, ULD Maximum available space within the container or pallet net envelope

International Air Transport Association (IATA)

An international trade and service organization for airlines of more than 100 countries serving international routes, IATA activities on behalf of shippers in international air freight include development of containerization programs, freight handling techniques and, for some airlines, uniform rates and rules.

International Civil Aviation Organization (ICAO)

The International Aviation Organization of Governments, ICAO is an agency of the United Nations. It was organized to insure orderly worldwide technical development of civil aviation.

International Organization for Standardization (ISO)

A worldwide federation of national standards organizations, "ISO container" denotes a container equipped with standard ISO corner fittings for lifting or for retaining on a truck chassis.

Joint Rate

A single through-rate on cargo moving via two or more air carriers or air and surface carriers

Just in Time (JIT)

The principle of production and inventory control that calls for immediate movement of raw materials, component parts, and work-in-progress. Goods arrive when needed (just in time) for production or use rather than becoming expensive inventory that occupies costly warehouse space.

Lay Order

The period during which the imported merchandise may remain at the place or unloading without some action being taken for its disposition, i.e., beyond the 5-day General Order period Length & Girth A limitation on shipment size occasionally used by an airline. The equation used to calculate length and girth: Length + (2 x width) + (2 x height). The largest measurement always used as the length in the equation.

Letter of Credit (LC)

A document issued by a bank at the request of the buyer of goods. The LC guarantees payment to the seller given receipt by the bank of certain shipping documents validating the delivery of goods, within a specified time period.

Load Factor, Cargo

The percentage of total available cargo capacity occupied by revenue cargo, it may be computer on the basis of volume, weight, or ULD capability.

Loading Gauge

A rigid framework in the shape of an airplane interior contour for the purpose of checking a pallet load on the ground to ensure it will fit into a particular position in a specific airplane type.

Loose Cargo, Loose Shipments

Air cargo delivered to an airline as separate packages and loaded and unloaded onto airplanes or unit of Loads (ULDs) by airline employees, and then delivered as separate pieces to the consigned.

Lot Labels

Labels attached to each piece of a multiple lot shipment for identification purposes.

Lower Deck

The compartment below the main deck (also called "lower love,' 'Lower hold,' 'pit' or 'belly').

Lower Deck Container/Pallet

A ULD shaped to fit the lower deck cargo compartment. These units come in half sizes and full sizes, related to the width across the airplane.

Main Deck Container/Pallet

A ULD carried on the main deck. These units come in half sizes and full sizes, related to the width across the airplane.

Marks Information placed on outer surface of shipping containers or packages such as address labels, box specifications, caution, or directional warnings.

Maximum Gross Payload On a cargo airplane, the maximum weight allowed and available for cargo. It includes the weight of the cargo, containers, pallets, straps and nets.

Maximum Gross Weight, ULD The maximum allowable combined weight of the ULD and its contents or payload.

Memorandum: Tariff Publications which contain rules and rate information extracted from official tariffs.

Memorandum tariffs are published by many carriers and are available from these carriers upon request.

Minimum Charge: The lowest rate applicable on each type of air cargo services no matter how small the shipment.

Non-structural Container

A unit load device composed of a bottomless rigid shell used in combination with a pallet and net assembly. Oversize Cargo Unusually large or heavy cargo that will not fit in the cargo areas of standard-body freighters or passenger airplanes, Cargo the exceeds the standard dimensions of common ULDs.

Pallet

A platform of standard dimensions on which goods are assembled and secured by nets and straps before being loaded as a unit onto an airplane. It has a flat under-surface to interface with ball, roller, or caster surfaces.

Pallet Net

A webbing or rope that can be secured to the pallet edges for restraining a pallet load. It may be used with a non-structural container.

Pickup and Delivery (PU&D)

An optional service for the surface transport of shipments from shipper's dock to origination air terminal and from the air terminal of destination to receiver's dock, for airfreight, an additional charge is usually assessed. It may be provide by an air freight forwarder, an integrated carrier, or by an independent truck operator either separately or under contract to an airline. Pivot Weight for shipments moving at container rates, it is the weight at which an additional charge is incurred for each pound over the picot weight. For shipments moving at bulk rates, the pivot weight is the weight at which it becomes less costly to pay the minimum charge at the higher weight break, than to pay for the actual weight at the lower weight break.

Prepaid Charges

The transportation trade practice under which the shipper pays transportation charges

Priority Air Freight

Those shipments that have first claim on available air transport capacity, transported at a premium charge.

Proof of Deliver (P.O.D.)

Information provide to payer containing the name of person who signed for the package with the date and time of delivery.

Protective Service

A protective service provided by airlines where shippers arrange to have a shipment under carrier surveillance that each stage of transit from origin to destination. The service may extend to pickup and delivery and may include armed guard protection. Restraint System The system installed in the floor of an airplane compartment that secures the ULD onto the floor to prevent its movement during flight. Also a net should be in front of the cargo load to protect the flight crew and/or passengers.

Restricted Articles

An out-dated term used to denote Dangerous Goods. This term is no longer used in regulations.

Road Feeder Service (RFS)

Freight service provided by the airlines using motor trucks, generally in conjunction with an air movement

Roller Ball Transfer

A conveyor system in an airplane or in terminal facilities consisting of various sizes of balls or rollers over which ULDs con be moved.

Seat Track

A standardized track on the main-deck of an airplane, designed to accept tie-down fittings. It is typically a continuous track capable of accepting tie-down fittings at any of the regularly spaced intervals provided.

Shell: A superstructure of any container or igloo.

Shipment One or more pieces of freight being transported under the contracted authority of one air waybill.

Signature Service

A service designed to provide continuous responsibility for the custody of shipments in transit, so named because a signature is required from each person handling the shipment at each stage of its transit form origin to destination.

Small Package Service

A specialized service guaranteeing the delivery of small parcels within specified express time limits, e.g. same day or next day. This traffic is subject to size and weight limitations. Most passenger air carriers also provide this service at airport ticket counters with delivery at destination baggage claim area. Often referred to as counter to counter

Special Rates

Rates that apply to traffic under special conditions in selected makers, Examples of such rates are Container rates, exception ratings, and surface-air rates.

Specific Commodity Rates (SCR)

Rates applicable to certain classes of commodities, usually these rates are applied to commodities that move in large volume shipments in a given market. Hence, specific commodity rates re usually lower than the general commodity rate between the same pair of cities.

Tare Weight

The actual weight of a container or pallet when empty, including all liners and/or fittings

Tare Weight Allowance

A free weight allowance given to shippers as part of a unitization incentive program for ULDs

Tariff

A document setting forth applicable rules, rates, and charges for the movement of goods, a tariff sets forth a contract of carriage for the shipper, the consignee, and the carrier. Tariffs are sometimes published by the carriers themselves and by a variety of publishing agencies, such as the Airline Tariff Publishing Company (ATPCO), The Air Cargo Tariff (TACT) and Cargo Rates Services, Inc. Thermal ULD A ULD built with insulating walls, doors, floor and roof which retard the rate of heat transmission between eh inside and the outside of the ULD.

Tie-down Strap

A strap which secures a load to the ULD or the airplane restraint system

Tracking/Tracing

A carriers system of following and recording movement intervals of shipments from origin to destination

Trailer

A towed vehicle with a roller platform for hauling ULDs between the cargo terminal and the airplane

Transit Air Cargo Manifest (TACM)

Procedures under which air cargo imports move through the gateway city to the city of final U.S. Customs destination for the collection of duty and other import processing.

Unitization

The practice or technique of consolidation many small pieces of freight into a single unit, usually through the use of aniline ULDs

Unit Load

A number of pieces of freight or cargo in a single box or container, or on a pallet held in place by a net, strapping, or similar device to make them suitable for transporting, stacking, or storage as a unit. It is also a single large item packaged for transporting, stacking, or storage.

Unit Load Device (ULD)

Term commonly used when referring to containers, pallets and pallet nets. The purpose of the ULD is to enable individual pieces of cargo to be assembled into standardized units to ease the rapid loading and unloading of airplanes and to facilitate the transfer of cargo between airplanes have compatible handling and restraint systems. Valuation Charges Transportation charges assessed shippers who declare a value of goods higher than the value of the carriers limits of liability.

Warsaw Convention

An international multilateral treaty which regulates, in a uniform manner, the conditions of international transportation by air, Among other things, it establishes the international liability of air carriers and establishers the monetary limits for loss, damage, and delay.

Weight and Balance Manual

Specific document for each airplane that controls the type and number of ULDs that can be loaded, their allowable weight and information on alternating loading arrangement

4.2 THE CONSOLIDATORS OR AIR FREIGHT FORWARDERS

i) Background and definition of a freight forwarder

Originally a commission agent acting on importer/exporter behalf

Routine tasks e.g. loading, unloading, customs brokerage, storage, local transport services

No standard definition of a freight forwarder

Prof. Alan E.Branch (2004) defines, "An entity or company responsible for undertaking export/import cargo arrangements on clients/shippers behalf at a seaport, airport and so on. At seaport it would include collection of freight; collection and issuing bills of lading; notification of arrival and loading of goods; customs, import & export documentation; certificates of shipment; arranging sorting of cargo, cold storage, warehousing, transport to destination including near continent; cargo or damage surveys; Lloyd's/marine agents surveys and so on. Also termed as forwarding agent.

ii) Freight Forwarder's role in International trade

Provides strategic solutions of long distance product sourcing and movement

Provides capabilities interfaced across a range of different transport modes

Offers supply chain management solutions

Delivery and customs clearance

Cargo handling and distribution management

Intermodal transport services

Consultancy/advisory services on international trade

Mega forwarders have increasingly enhanced their role by adapting to changing global logistics scene and investing heavily in information technology and quality trained committed staff.

iii) Relationship to the Industry

Relationship with:

Government and other Public Authorities

Consignor

Consignee

Cargo Insurers

Carriers and other agencies

Port Authorities

Scope of Services

i) On behalf of the Consignor or Exporter

In accordance with exporter shipping instructions the forwarder would:

Book space with carrier

Choose route

Take delivery

Arrange warehousing

Note damages/loss Weigh and measure cargo

Advice on insurance

Monitor cargo movement

Study letter of credit L/C provisions

Transport the goods

Pay fees and other charges

Attend to foreign exchange transactions

Arrange for transhipment

ii) On behalf of the Consignee

- Receive and verify relevant documents
- Monitor cargo movement
- Take delivery
- Arrange customs clearance
- Assist in pursuing claims
- Warehousing and distribution

iii) Other Value Added Services

iv) Special Cargoes e.g project cargo, garment hanging services, overseas exhibition

v) Inventory and Supply Chain Management

Air cargo airlines and airlines which carry a portion of freight traffic contribute to the larger courier service industry, which, simply put, delivers messages, packages, and mail. Air freight is a small portion of a much larger logistics networks which involve production, packaging, material handling, inventory, transportation, warehousing, security, and information flow. In the supply chain, customers include end–consumers, retailers, and businesses. These customers contract logistics to shippers, forwarders, or integrators who then select relevant modes of transportation to ship the good. Modes include air, water, and ground transportation. The end package then becomes delivered to the consignee. As a form of transportation, air freight remains just one option out of many. In fact, the growth of the air cargo industry resulted in contributions to the trucking industry, because air freight often feeds into regional trucking as the end mode of transportation. There are different characteristics in terms of operations, delivery, and economics at play between the different modes.

4.3 SERVICE FUNCTIONS

Functions and Tasks for: "Cargo and Freight Agent"

1. Check import or export documentation to determine cargo contents, and classify goods into different fee or tariff groups, using a tariff coding system.
2. Contact vendors and/or claims adjustment departments in order to resolve problems with shipments, or contact service depots to arrange for repairs.
3. Determine method of shipment, and prepare bills of lading, invoices, and other shipping documents.
4. Direct delivery trucks to shipping doors or designated marshalling areas, and help load and unload goods safely.
5. Direct or participate in cargo loading in order to ensure completeness of load and even distribution of weight.
6. Enter shipping information into a computer by hand or by using a hand-held scanner that reads bar codes on goods.

7. Estimate freight or postal rates, and record shipment costs and weights.
8. Inspect and count items received and check them against invoices or other documents, recording shortages and rejecting damaged goods.
9. Keep records of all goods shipped, received, and stored.
10. Negotiate and arrange transport of goods with shipping or freight companies.
11. Notify consignees, passengers, or customers of the arrival of freight or baggage, and arrange for delivery.
12. Retrieve stored items and trace lost shipments as necessary.
13. Route received goods to first available flight or to appropriate storage areas or departments, using forklifts, hand-trucks, or other equipment.
14. Assemble containers and crates used to transport items such as machines or vehicles.
15. Attach address labels, identification codes, and shipping instructions to containers.
16. Coordinate and supervise activities of workers engaged in packing and shipping merchandise.
17. Inspect trucks and vans to ensure cleanliness when shipping such items as grain, flour, and milk.
18. Install straps, braces, and padding to loads in order to prevent shifting or damage during shipment.
19. Maintain a supply of packing materials.
20. Obtain flight numbers, airplane numbers, and names of crew members from dispatchers, and record data on airplane flight papers.
21. Open cargo containers and unwrap contents, using steel cutters, crowbars, or other hand tools.

22. Pack goods for shipping, using tools such as staplers, strapping machines, and hammers.
23. Position ramps for loading of airplanes.
24. Prepare manifests showing baggage, mail, and freight weights, and number of passengers on airplanes, and transmit data to destinations.
25. Arrange insurance coverage for goods.
26. Remove ramps after airplane loading is complete, and signal pilots that personnel and equipment are clear of plane.
27. Shovel loose materials into machine hoppers or into vehicles and containers.
28. Force conditioned air into interiors of planes prior to departure, using mobile aircraft-air-conditioning-units.
29. Send samples of merchandise to quality control units for inspection.
30. Advise clients on transportation and payment methods.

4.4 CARGO LIABILITY

The definition of cargo liability insurance is insurance that protects products that are in transit by ship, train, and semitrailer truck or delivery vehicle. An example of cargo liability insurance is what would protect a shipment of cars on a semitrailer truck against theft or damage while en route to a dealership.

Carriers' Liability Insurance

The carrier may consider the following factors in determining how to choose to manage its risk:

- The size of the carrier, as measured by such factors as gross revenues, net current asset position, or net worth to total assets ratio;

- The loss experience of the carrier, as determined by the distribution and frequency of cargo claims by size, their predictability, and any identifiable trends;
- Other issues relating to insurance and risk management, for example, the cash management policy of the carrier, the overall long term total costs of claims and insurance, the current quotations for insurance at different deductibles, and the costs of providing claims services in-house.
- The legal regime under which it must operate, including the defences to, and limitations on liability.

There is no direct link between the carrier's liability insurer and the shipper unless one is established by statute or regulation. For instance, pursuant to regulation, a carrier's liability insurance contract requires that in the event of a motor carrier's bankruptcy, the liability insurer must pay all valid claims, including the deductible. In this case the claimant would clearly have the direct benefit of the carrier's liability policy.

Current issues in cargo liability

The primary framework for discussion of issues in this chapter will be the factors and criteria which the International Council of Chemical Trade Association (ICCTA) requires the Secretary of Transportation to consider for this study of cargo liability. They are:

a. Efficient delivery of transportation services
b. International harmony
c. Intermodal harmony
d. The public interest
e. The interests of carriers, and
f. The interests of shippers.

g. Limitation of liability particular emphasis was given to this criterion, which will be discussed in the context of the liability regime.

Basically, a cargo liability regime is a method for allocating the risk of carriage. In theory, the entire risk of carriage could exclusively be allocated either to the carrier or the shipper.

In practice, such a unilateral risk allocation would remove the incentive for the shipper or carrier to be careful in handling the goods. Such unilateral risk allocation is neither good tort law nor is it in the public interest. Consequently, it is the view of DOT that both shippers and carriers should bear a burden of responsibility that provides incentive for and is in accord with their self-interest in careful and successful completion of transportation, without loss, damage, or delay.

Five defenses to liability

The U.S. Supreme Court case of Missouri Pacific RR Co. v. Elmore & Stahl, 377 U.S. 134 (1964), held that the Act codifies the common law that a carrier is liable for the cargo transported, unless the carrier can prove that the loss or damage was caused by any of the following five defenses:

a. Act of God: This defense is defined as an event which occurred without intervention of a human being or one that could not be prevented by exercise of human care. Lightning would be an example of an Act of God. The carrier would remain liable if its negligence mingled with the Act of God.37 Because an Act of God is outside the influence of either the carrier or the shipper, any change in this defense would not affect safety or efficiency of carriage. Thus this study does not recommend a change to the defense.

b. Act of the Public Enemy: The defense known as "act of public enemy" involves an event which is outside the influence of either the carrier or the shipper. This defense may be invoked if loss, damage or delay is caused by an enemy military force. No change in safety or efficiency would occur by a change in this defense. Consequently no change is recommended.

c. Act of the Shipper Himself: This defense may be invoked by the carrier if the shipper fails to pack or load the freight properly. The carrier must prove that the shipper's act was the sole cause of the loss or damage and that the carrier was not contributory negligent. The test is: what is the cause of the loss or damage? Only if the shipper's negligence was the sole cause of the loss and damage does the carrier escape liability.

d. Act of a Public Authority: This defense may be used, for example, if public authorities, such as the police, seize the cargo as evidence in a criminal prosecution. This defense is rarely invoked.

e. Loss or Damage by Inherent Vice or Nature of the Goods: Missouri Pacific RR Co. v.

Elmore and Stahl, 377 U.S. 134, 136 (1964) explains the defense of inherent vice as being based on "existing defects, diseases, decay or the inherent nature of the commodity which will cause it to deteriorate with a lapse of time.

4.5 AIR CARGO ACCEPTANCE

ACCEPTANCE

Perishable cargoes should be accepted for shipment only if it is known for certain that the cargo will arrive to destination in good condition.

Cargo consignor should present written instructions concerning the maximum accepted time of shipment and any specially required procedure of processing. These instructions should be specified in the waybill and with cargo packages.

Before acceptance the carrier should make sure that all necessary preparations on shipment routing are made, incl.:

Guarantee that the cargo consignor is informed about maximal time before a flight departure during which the carrier will accept a cargo;

Implementation of any necessary further booking procedures;

Guarantee that special procedures of processing such as refreezing are accessible and are carried out, if they are stipulated and required.

IATA label "Perishable cargoes" should be attached to each cargo package; there also should be a label "Top" where necessary.

4.5.1 Instructions for Carriage

Acceptance of Cargo for Carriage

1. Value Limits for One Aircraft

The carrier determines the limit of the value of a consignment or a group of consignments which may be carried in one single aircraft. If any individual consignment exceeds such limit, it may not be carried in one aircraft but is apportioned to two or several aircrafts at the carrier's due discretion. The carrier is entitled to deny the carriage of consignments in one aircraft if the declared total value would lead to a violation of this principle.

2. Packaging and Labeling of the Cargo; Declaration of Value

a. The consignor shall package the cargo for safe carriage by air in a manner suitable to protect it against loss, damage or deterioration and preventing personal injury or damage to property. Consignments at risk from robbery or theft shall be neutrally packaged without indication of their contents. Each packing unit must bear the name and full postal address of both consignor and consignee in a legible and permanent manner and it must be marked with the necessary information for the carriage.

b. Hazardous materials must be marked as such in accordance with applicable laws and regulations. If accepted for carriage, the consignor shall send hazardous materials as well as valuable cargo or live animals by the carriage form provided for the carriage of such cargo by the carrier, including the surcharge published for such case.

c. Temperature-sensitive cargo including but not limited to pharmaceuticals must be packaged in accordance with the special characteristics of the cargo and in a way that guarantees adequate protection against heat, which could potentially damage the cargo. This includes sending the cargo in sufficient transport containers e.g. cool containers where appropriate for an additional fee and in sufficient means of transportation. The provision of specific transport containers by the carrier shall not affect the applicability of any international conventions.

d. With regard to each handing over of cargo for carriage, the consignor may state (particularly declare) its interest in delivery to the place of destination in figures and to pay the requested surcharge.

e. In the event of cash on delivery consignments, the consignor shall legibly write the letters Cash On Delivery "C.O.D." on each individual packing item, in addition to the names and addresses of both consignor and consignee.

4.5.2 Acceptance Based on the Shipper's Letter of Instructions (SLI)

Shipper's Letter of Instruction is a document, which provides shipping instructions to the shipper's freight forwarder to ensure accurate and correct movement of their products across borders. Often this document will include billing terms regarding the freight and other charges as well as documentation preparation, instructions in cases where the shipper is not providing those documents. In some cases product distribution instructions are also included.

When it comes to preparing export paperwork, the Shipper's Letter of Instruction (SLI) is one document that many exporters are unexplainably reluctant to prepare. They shouldn't be.

By completing an SLI and sending it to the freight forwarder, you are establishing a best practice for your firm. You have a written record of who received the shipping documents, who to contact for questions, which to contact for proof of export, and who issued the export control documentation that supports the decision to send your products to your foreign customer.

While there are several reasons to create an SLI, here are the top five:

The exporter has a written record of its instructions to the forwarder;

It acts as the request for documents prepared by the freight forwarder, including the relevant Electronic Export Information (EEI) extract, any other export control documents, and the international bill of lading;

It provides the data elements that are required for filing the EEI as specified in the Foreign Trade Regulations (FTR), amended 2014;

If you are authorized to provide the freight forwarder with a written power of attorney, it includes this provision for the USPPI along with a signature line; and the format you use can be modified by you and your team to include additional data or instructions.

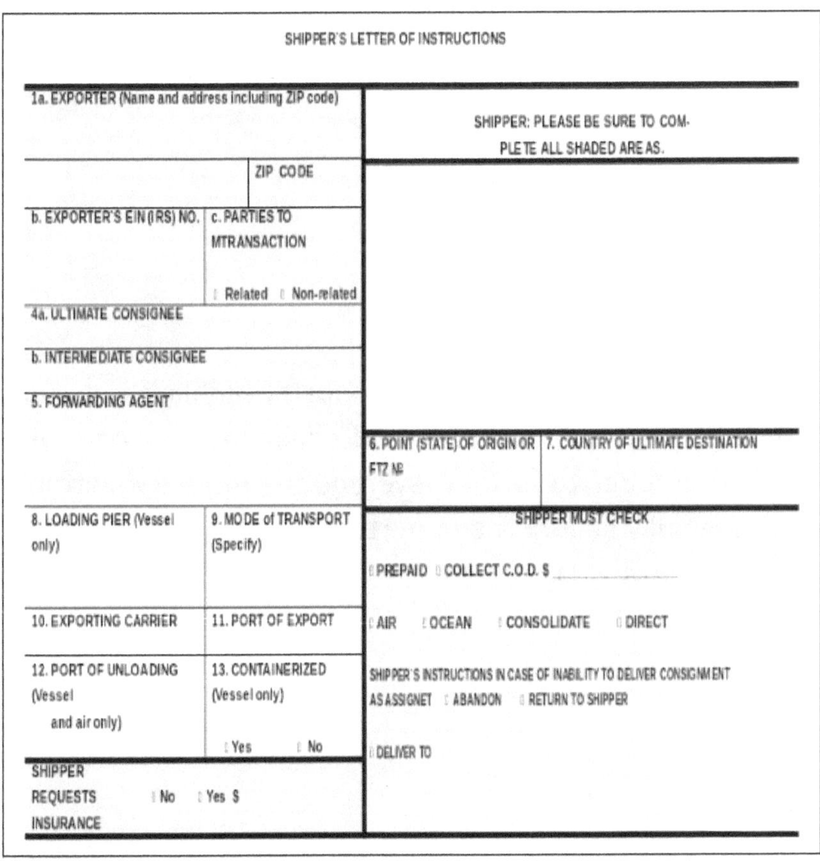

SHIPPER'S LETTER OF INSTRUCTIONS

1a. EXPORTER (Name and address including ZIP code)		SHIPPER: PLEASE BE SURE TO COMPLETE ALL SHADED AREAS.
	ZIP CODE	
b. EXPORTER'S EIN (IRS) NO.	c. PARTIES TO TRANSACTION Related Non-related	
4a. ULTIMATE CONSIGNEE		
b. INTERMEDIATE CONSIGNEE		
5. FORWARDING AGENT		6. POINT (STATE) OF ORIGIN OR FTZ N° | 7. COUNTRY OF ULTIMATE DESTINATION
8. LOADING PIER (Vessel only)	9. MODE of TRANSPORT (Specify)	SHIPPER MUST CHECK PREPAID COLLECT C.O.D. $ ______
10. EXPORTING CARRIER	11. PORT OF EXPORT	AIR OCEAN CONSOLIDATE DIRECT
12. PORT OF UNLOADING (Vessel and air only)	13. CONTAINERIZED (Vessel only) Yes No	SHIPPER'S INSTRUCTIONS IN CASE OF INABILITY TO DELIVER CONSIGNMENT AS ASSIGNED ABANDON RETURN TO SHIPPER DELIVER TO
SHIPPER REQUESTS INSURANCE No Yes $		

Figure 3: Shipper's Letter of Instructions
Source: www.template.net

4.6 SPECIAL CARGO

Special Cargo" means the Cargo which needs special attention in course of its acceptance, storage, transport and delivery due to its nature, value or other conditions.

In today's air cargo environment customers expect carriers to ship any type of commodity that is why Air Cargo department has been consistently developing special cargo delivery options gleaning its experience, nailing down its handling procedures and expertise and certifying its personnel to guarantee the level of quality service for customers are accustomed to:

i) *Dangerous Goods*
ii) *Perishable Products*
iii) *Human remains*
iv) *Oversize& heavy*
v) *Live Animals*
vi) *Oil & Gas*

A SWOT analysis of the air cargo industry highlights a number of very significant weaknesses and challenges which must be addressed in order to further leverage the industry's strengths and successfully secure the opportunities that will arise.

Strengths	Weaknesses
Largest temperature-controlled aircraft container company Quality of services and product which are in alignment with the user requirements New technology ensures efficient cool chain management and unbroken cool chains Enhanced product durability, due to the use of advanced materials Enhanced handling capability (fork-liftable containers) Global presence and capability of manufacturing – support companies Relationships with key industry stakeholders Extensive experience and expertise	Conventional ULDs are potentially more expendable compared to advanced ULDs Repair and support cost unknown Acquisition cost is high Complexity requires specialised labour and technical know-how which may remain with the manufacturer Uni-directional nature of air cargo traffic (Vega, 2008). could pose re-positioning issues for the containers
Opportunities	**Threats**
Capability to cover emerging markets, for example, South America Increased outreach of perishable medical supplies in hard to reach geographically dispersed areas Opportunities for other value added perishables, such as local products, for example, chilled salmon Globalisation of the pharmaceutical industry Ageing of the world population and advances in pharmaceuticals for treatment	Advances in maritime containers technology and cheaper ocean freight costs could result in firms switching from air to ocean transport modes Reliance upon the pharmaceutical sector growth – may be affected by external factors New ULD manufacturers could enter the market

Figure 4: A SWOT Analysis
Source: qualityinspection.org

Conclusion

The transport of commercial cargo is a key economic indicator of international trade and the state of the global economy. The supply chain and logistics industry exists to connect manufacturer of goods to end customers who are willing to pay for these services and goods. The air cargo segment is just one link in an entire system designed to market and transport goods across the globe. Characteristics of goods shipped by air include time as the key value being added. The quick delivery of key items or packages results in a higher priced demand because customers are more willing to pay for goods that are delivered fast and on time. Common goods shipped by air include electronics and clothing. Cargo is carried by both Combination Carriers, which carry both passenger and cargo, and All Cargo Airlines. The first all-cargo airlines were founded on the basis that dual optimization of both passengers and cargo is not optimal. The cargo industry and passenger airline industry share many of the same features in operating aircraft and fundamental business models such as the network hub and spoke orientation.

Chapter 5

Cargo Booking Procedures

The air cargo airlines remain distinct from passenger-based airlines through underlying constraints on efficiency as well as bureaucratic impositions. For safety reasons for example, cargo planes in the United States are forbidden from carrying non-crew and non-employee passengers. The handling agent will often be a separate company contracted by the airline, but cargo handling can also be an in-house function of the airline, especially at a major hub. The airlines often offer their in-house cargo handling as a commercial service to other airlines.

The handling agent takes care of the air cargo at the airport, to and from the aircraft. Depending on the kind of goods, destination or flight number and urgency, delivery at the handling agent has to be done within a certain norm-time before departure (TBD) of the aircraft, also called a slot or a slot-time.

Whether a direct or a transit process should be used is up to the forwarder where necessary in communication with the shipper and depends on required price, through put-time also in relation to flight schedules of different airlines or special cargo requirements such as security, live animals, etc.

Besides the physical handling, other important functions of the handling agent are:

> ➢ To control the overall weight & balance of the airline's aircraft on the cargo side, make a load sheet and assure flight safety

> To make a cargo manifest for all the goods on board, for the airline's import and export declaration to customs. This is a high level customs declaration as opposed to detailed customs declaration by the forwarder or customs agent
> To make a notification to the captain of the aircraft (NOTOC) to inform the crew about potential risks of the cargo on board in case of emergencies of dangerous goods, live animals, valuables, etc., as well as for the right conditioning or temperature of the cargo holds
> To plan & control bookings, slot-times, goods flows in the warehouse, and ULD and flight bag flows from and to the aircraft in order to prevent delays and assure correct execution of the airline's time-table
> To plan & control worldwide ULD stock

The incoming checks before loading and departure of the aircraft are of vital importance for the airline as well as rest of the process:

Commercial checks

- According to booking
- Correct weights, numbers and volumes of colli indicated

Logistics checks

- Delivered Request For Comments(RFC)

Flight safety checks

- Correct weights, numbers and volumes of colli indicated
- Correct and undamaged packaging
- Potentially hazardous materials declared and correctly labelled and visible
- Correct and complete documents and labels

Security checks

- Known shipper and forwarder declared
- Correct and undamaged packaging
- Correct and complete documents and labels

Booking

The first step after the pricing is obtained, is to make an airline booking for the shipment and get the airline's confirmation in order to assure space on board of an aircraft:

- Airline (Master) Air Waybill number assigned
- Origin and (final) destination
- Type of goods/commodity (especially important for dangerous goods, perishables and valuables)
- Flight date
- Flight number
- Weight, volume and dimensions of shipment
- Number of colli
- Issuing agent/contact details
- Eventual assignment to customer (agent's) allotment

The reservation will be validated against the airline's capacity, commodity and revenue management criteria, and will be officially confirmed as soon as the booking is accepted. Now the booking process is complete

5.1 CARGO AND AIRLINE BOOKING PROCEDURES

Air Cargo Handling Services

When selecting an air cargo carrier to handle air cargo shipments, consider the requirements in terms of the following services and make carrier selection based on the range of services that will meet the requirements:

Import Air Freight and Export Air Freight.

- Receipt and check-in of shipments
- Storage of shipments by certified personnel for accepting dangerous goods
- Document handling Cargo labelling services
- Collection services Palletize/unitize shipments for air carriage
- Record keeping Air waybill/flight manifest preparation
- Knowledge of Compliance issues, regulations
- Airline equipment storage and inventory maintenance
- Ability to handle perishables scheduling and interlining considerations
- Convenient Scheduling Ability to handle perishables
- Tracking and Tracing Tracking and Tracing
- Consolidation Services Consolidation Services
- Small Parcel Services Small Parcel Services
- Notification upon arrival Notification to consignees upon arrival
- Air Cargo Handling Equipment

A variety of equipment is available through your air cargo carrier for moving and weighing Unit Loading Device (ULD) pallets and containers. The following chart demonstrates the range of conveying systems and ramp equipment used to convey goods on and off the aircraft:

Conveying systems

- i) dock lifts
- ii) powered conveyors
- iii) Gravity conveyors
- iv) elevating conveyors

   v)   Ball mats

  vi)   Right angle transfer decks

 vii)   Turntables

viii)   Workstations

  ix)   Scales

   x)   control systems

Ramp Equipment

   i)   Aircraft loaders

  ii)   Fly-away loader adapters

 iii)   Cargo trailers

 iv)   Cargo baggage carts

5.2 THE OAG CARGO GUIDE

The OAG Cargo Guide Worldwide gives cargo agents, freight forwarders and commercial/business shipper's comprehensive coverage of worldwide air cargo schedules. It's the essential tool for moving goods quickly and efficiently from their point of production to their point of sale. The Cargo Guide is comprised of reference publications for airfreight professionals, containing worldwide information on moving freight by air.

The OAG is published monthly; the Cargo Guide also offers essential information like public holidays in nations worldwide, documentation requirements and other cargo-related details.

A yearly subscription includes 12 monthly issues plus the bi-annual Cargo Guide Rules Supplement with regulations by country, documentary requirements, aircraft loading restrictions, and much more.

Key features of OAG Cargo Guide

 i) Updated monthly.
 ii) More than 68,000 cargo flights.
 iii) Yearly subscription includes the Bi-annual Cargo Guide Rules
 iv) Supplement with regulations by country, documentary requirements, and aircraft loading restrictions.
 v) Selected airport to airport truck services.
 vi) Documentation requirements and other cargo-related details.
 vii) Public holiday listings for nations worldwide
 viii) Cargo and passenger carriers
 ix) Regulations by country
 x) Aircraft loading restrictions.

5.3 FUNCTIONS OF THE AIRWAY BILL

The *Air Waybill* (*AWB*) is the contract of carriage between the 'shipper' (e.g. forwarder) and the 'carrier' (airline).

A shipping document used by the airlines for air freight. It serves as a contract for carriage and includes carrier conditions of carriage such as limits of liability and claims procedures. The air waybill also contains shipping instructions to the airline, a description of the commodity, and applicable transportation charges. The airline industry has adopted a standard formatted air waybill that accommodates both domestic and international traffic.

The receipt issued by an airline or its agent for the carriage of goods is called air way bill or air consignment note.

Functions

There are several purposes that an air waybill serves, but its main functions are:

1. *Contract of Carriage:* Behind every original of the Air Waybill are conditions of contract for carriage.
2. *Evidence of Receipt of Goods*: When the shipper delivers goods to be forwarded, he will get a receipt. The receipt is proof that the shipment was handed over in good order and condition and also that the shipping instructions, as contained in the Shipper's Letter of Instructions, are acceptable.
3. *Freight Bill*: The air waybill may be used as a bill or invoice together with supporting documents since it may indicate charges to be paid by the consignee, charges due to the agent or the carrier. An original copy of the air waybill is used for the carrier's accounting
4. *Certificate of Insurance:* the air waybill may also serve as evidence if the carrier is in a position to insure the shipment and is requested to do so by the shipper.
5. *Customs Declaration:* Although customs authorities require various documents like a commercial invoice, packing list, etc. the air waybill too is proof of the freight amount billed for the goods carried and may be needed to be presented for customs clearance Usually, airline air waybills are distributed to IATA cargo agents by IATA airlines.

The air waybills show:

- the carrier's name
- its head office address
- its logo
- the pre-printed eleven digit air waybill number

6. Air Waybill Number: the AWB number has 11 digits and 3 parts.

   + The first 3 digits are the Airline Prefix
   + The next 7 digits is the Serial Number of the AWB
   + The last digit is the Check digit. The industry is now transitioning from the use of the paper AWB to the electronic AWB (e-AWB).

7. Air way bill format
8. Air way bill receipt
9. Section Instructions
   1. Fill in sender information, including your FedEx account number.
   2. Record any internal numbers or codes you need for reference.
   3. Be sure to include the recipient's phone number, along with other accurate information. In some cases the recipient's tax I.D. number is required for Customs purposes.

5.4 PRINCIPAL REQUIREMENTS FOR AN AIRWAY BILL

The air waybill is a document which shall be either an air waybill referred to as an "airline air waybill", with preprinted issuing carrier identification, or an air waybill referred to as a "neutral air waybill" without preprinted identification of the issuing carrier in any form and used by other than an air carrier.

Measurements of the Air Waybill

The outside measurements of the air waybill shall be between 208 mm (8.2 in) and 230 mm (9 in) in width and between 274 mm (10.8 in) and 305 mm (12 in) in length. The size of the boxes and their distances from the upper left hand paper edges shall be maintained exactly as shown in attachment.

Description of the airline Air Waybill set

The airline air waybill set shall be printed as specified below:

The Original 3 for Shipper shall have the same layout, wording and shading

The Copy 4, Delivery Receipt, shall have the same layout, wording and shading.

The Original 1 for Issuing Carrier and Original 2 for Consignee shall have the same layout, wording and shading

All other copies shall have the same layout, wording and shading

The airline air waybill shall be in a set of a minimum of eight copies and shall be marked in the order shown. Colour is optional and airlines shall accept both coloured and non-coloured coded air waybills.

Title Colour

Original 3 (for Shipper) – Blue

Copy 8 (for Agent) – White

Original 1 (for Issuing Carrier) – Green

Original 2 (for Consignee) – Pink

Copy 4 (Delivery Receipt) – Yellow

Copy 5 (Extra Copy) – White

Copy 6 (Extra Copy) – White

Copy 7 (Extra Copy) – White

If using colour, copies shall be either coloured paper or white paper with appropriate colour ink imprinted thereon, as referred above. Additional copies, having the same layout, wording and shading, may be included in the airline.

Air waybill set to a maximum of five copies. These must be printed on white paper marked "Copy XX , Extra copy for Carrier", where XX denotes the number of the copy of the airline air waybill, and may be placed anywhere in the airline air waybill set following Original 1 for Issuing Carrier;

Notwithstanding the provisions of 3.5 and 3.6, when an air carrier uses an automated system to issue the airline air waybill:

The airline air waybill shall be executed in a set which includes at least the three original copies, further copies of the airline air waybill may be produced by automated means at origin, en route or at destination as required,

upon interline transfer, at least five copies, of which one copy is entitled "Original 2 for Consignee" and one copy is entitled "Copy 4 Delivery Receipt", shall be provided to the onward carrier, upon interline transfer,

When the exchange of a shipment record is not possible, at least five copies, of which one copy is entitled "Original 2 ,for Consignee" and one copy is entitled "Copy 4 ,Delivery Receipt,", shall be provided to the onward carrier,

When the exchange of a shipment record is possible, it is not required that copies of an air waybill be provided to the onward carrier.

5.5 DIFFERENCE BETWEEN AIRWAY BILL AND BILL OF LOADING

Airway bill is issued by air carrier of goods on receipt of goods after completion of export customs formalities of the country. Shipper obtains airway bill once after handing over cargo to them. Since the cargo reaches by air and transit time is too less compared to sea shipment, a set of airway bill is sent along with the cargo for immediate reference on transit and for import customs clearance at destination port by importer. Once after completion of customs formalities at load port customs location, cargo transfer manifest (CTM) issued by IATA agent along with airway bill and other required documents for transportation submits to air carriers. Original airway bills are issued in quintuplicate which is meant for carrier, importer, shipper and additional copies. Once after arrival of cargo at destination, the importer or his cargo agent approaches the destination office of air carrier and collect airway bill and other required documents sent by shipper along with cargo for necessary documentation for import customs clearance procedures and other references. Importer may also collect copies of documents by courier or mail from shipper before arrival of goods.

The shipper also can arrange to send airway bill and other documents through his bank to meet letter of credit (LC) requirements or he desires.

Bill of landing (B/L) is a transport document, which is used in port-to-port sea shipments, issued and signed by liner carrier or its agent, generally on a pre-printed carrier's bill of lading format, evidences the terms and conditions of the carriage of goods between port of loading and port of discharge.

The major difference between bill of lading and Airway bill is that, Airway bill is not a document of title. However, airway bill can be prepared in such a way to treat as document of title and negotiable document.

The main features of a bill of lading (B/L)

Negotiable bill of lading represents and gives title to the goods and normally has to be surrendered at the port of discharge to the carrier's agent to obtain delivery of the goods.

Bill of lading issued and signed by the carrier or an agent on behalf of the carrier. Alternatively it can be issued and signed by a freight forwarder. But carrier bill of lading and forwarder bill of lading are not the same documents.

A bill of loading generally issued subject to Hague Rules, The Hague-Visby Rules and US COGSA (US Carriage of Goods by Sea Act 1936.) etc.

Bill of loading should be used in port-to-port sea shipments, as a result only it can be used in conjunction with all types of incoterms.

Air waybill (AWB) is a transport document, which is used in air shipments, issued and signed by an airline cargo carrier or its agent, generally on a pre-printed air waybill format, evidences the terms and conditions of the carriage of goods over routes of the airline carrier(s).

BILL OF LOADING – COMMERCIAL

Carrier will furnish commercial bill of loading sets required by the Government without any additional charge. The bill of loading sets can consist of any number of copies.

BILL OF LOADING – CORRECTED

(1) Corrected bills of loading, or other written instructions from the consignor to change the freight charge collection status from "COLLECT" to "PREPAID", may be accepted only if received by the origin carrier within a period of 30 days from the date of the initial bill of lading.

(2) Corrected bills of lading other written instructions to change the freight collection status from "PREPAID" to "COLLECT" will not be accepted once the shipment has been delivered.

(3) A corrected bill of lading or other written instructions to change the original transportation contract from "PREPAID" to "COLLECT" will not be accepted if Section 7 of the corrected bill of lading has been signed by the consignor.

The main features of an air waybill (AWB)

Air waybill, contrary to bill of lading, is not a document of title, as a result it is not a negotiable document. Carriers' agents deliver goods by approving the identity of the consignee without requesting surrender of the original air waybill.

Air Waybill is not a negotiable document as a result it cannot be issued .An air waybill can only be consigned to a "named company".

Air waybill issued and signed by the carrier or an agent on behalf of the carrier. Alternatively it can be issued and signed by a freight forwarder. But carrier air waybill and forwarder air waybill are not the same documents. Air waybills are generally issued subject to Warsaw Convention, Hague amendment, Montreal Convention, etc.

Air waybill should be used in airport-to-airport shipments; as a result it cannot be used in conjunction with the incoterms available only sea shipments such as Free alongside Ship (FAS), Free On Board (FOB) and cost net insured (CIF).

An Air Waybill, also known as an air consignment note refers to a receipt issued by an international courier company for goods. Air Waybills make sure that goods have been received for shipment by air. Every Air waybill has a tracking number that is used to check the status of a delivery and current position of the shipment. A typical air waybill sample consists of three originals and nine copies.

The goods in the air consignment are consigned directly to the party (the consignee) named in the letter of credit (L/C). Unless the goods are consigned to a third party like the issuing bank, the importer can obtain the goods from the carrier at destination without paying the issuing bank or the consignor. Therefore, unless a cash payment has been received by the exporter or the buyer's integrity is unquestionable; consigning goods directly to the importer is risky.

For air consignment to certain destinations, it is possible to arrange payment on a COD (cash on delivery) basis and consign the goods directly to the importer. The goods are released to the importer only after the importer makes the payment and complies with the instructions in the AWB.

AWB must indicate that the goods have been accepted for carriage, and it must be signed or authenticated by the carrier or the named agent for or on behalf of the carrier.

The principal requirements for an Air Waybill are:

- ➢ The proper shipper and consignee must be mentioned.
- ➢ The airport of departure and destination must be mentioned.
- ➢ The descriptions of goods must be consistent with that shown on other documents.
- ➢ Any weight, measure or shipping marks must agree with those shown on other documents.
- ➢ It must be signed and dated by the actual carrier or by the named agent of a named carrier. It must mention whether freight has been paid or will be paid at the destination point.
- ➢ All air waybills are non-negotiable. A waybill is very similar to a Bill of Lading in that it performs the functions of a cargo receipt and contract of carriage.

Both Bill of Lading (B/L) and Waybill are among the most important documents in international trade.

The key difference between a B/L and a Waybill is that a waybill does not convey title. The cargo named on the waybill can be released only to the named consignee and NO ORIGINAL documents are required. The consignee needs only to identify himself.

If a Bill of Lading is issued, the consignee can receive the cargo only when the original documents are presented.

5.6 LABELLING AND MARKING

The correct marking of packages helps to prevent incorrect handling and delivery, accidents, losses of weight and volume and Customs fines. Marking must be clear. Its colour should stand out clearly from that of the package.

When marking is applied directly onto the package and when adhesive labels are used, care must be taken to ensure that marking is applied in a legible and durable manner. All packages should have markings on three sides.

5.7 MARKS GROUPINGS

MARKS

The primary purpose of marking is the identification of the shipment, enabling the carrier to forward it to the ultimate consignee. Old marks, advertising and other extraneous information only serve to confuse this primary function for cargo handlers and carriers.

Follow these fundamental marking rules:

1. Unless local regulations prohibit, use coded marks; particularly where goods are susceptible to pilferage. Change them periodically to avoid familiarity by cargo handlers. Trade names should be avoided as they may indicate the nature of the contents.

2. Consignee (identification) marks and port marks showing destination and transfer points should be large, clear and applied by stencil with waterproof ink. They should be applied on three faces of the package, preferably side, and/or ends and top.

3. If commodities require special handling or stowage, the shipping package should be so marked, and this information should also appear on the bill of lading.

4. Cautionary and handling markings must be permanent and easy to read (use the languages of both the origin and destination countries). The use of stencils is recommended for legibility do not use crayon, tags, or cards.

5.8 PACKAGING AND MARKING

The ADR specifies the correct way to package dangerous goods, be it in a box, drum, container, or when carried in road tankers or other systems of containment. Packaging provides a safeguard for people and the environment during loading, transport and unloading of dangerous goods and must therefore be appropriate for the dangerous goods concerned.

Basic Markings

Normally packaging holding dangerous goods are marked with:

- ➢ Proper Shipping Name
- ➢ Identification Number
- ➢ Technical Name if required

Additional Markings

These markings include:

- ➢ The Marine Pollutant Marking if the material is a marine pollutant. (Exceptions exist for small packages)
- ➢ Limited Quantity Mark when the quantity meets the criteria of the Dangerous Goods List
- ➢ Orientation Arrows to be placed on two opposite sides of combination packaging containing liquid dangerous goods

Marking and Labelling of Dangerous Goods

Dangerous goods packages must be marked and labelled before they are assigned for shipment. The differences between marking and labelling under Transportation of Dangerous Goods (TDG) are listed as below:

Marking: mainly refers to UN number, proper shipping names, UN specification marks and other markings if applicable i.e.

orientation arrows, environmental hazardous substances mark for UN 3077 and UN 3082 and excepted quantities mark;

Labelling: mainly means hazard symbols and handling labels displayed on small means of packages usually less than 450 litres.

Limited Quantity and Excepted Quantity Marking

Selected dangerous goods packed in small quantities or very small volumes excepted quantity pose a lesser risk in transport than do the same goods packed in larger volumes. Thus they qualify for some relief from robust packaging requirements provided that they are packed and marked properly. This could save considerable packaging costs.

Packing requirements

Wood treatment

All solid wood, used for packing including wooden pallets and/or stowage and fumigation according to the international standard ISPM 15 (IPPC), latest version. As these rules are not the same for all countries, the procedure is to be met for the country of final destination. If the supplier is not aware of the country of final destination he has the obligation to inform himself. Use of untreated wood is not acceptable.

Pallets

When equipment and/or materials are packed on pallets wood or synthetic, these should be solid double deck pallets that provide adequate load support during transportation and storage under not always ideal conditions.

The pallets should have a dynamic load capacity, enough to carry the mass loaded on the pallet.

Where feasible, the top surface of the pallet must be flat. The pallet design must enable safe handling by forklift, cranes etc. and storage on rough surface.

Packaging

All equipment and materials shall be properly fixed by bolts, clamps, supporting beams, etc. in such a way that internal movements and/or working loose will be impossible. Under the top cover or roof depending on the case and crate length, a sufficient number of strong beams shall be placed and properly fixed in order to allow stacking of the cases and crates while avoiding any compression.

Equipment parts and materials which may be subject to damage by vibration and/or shock must be protected using shock-absorbing material.

All openings on the equipment must be closed with wooden or plastic covers to prevent damage to the openings and interiors. Fragile and loose parts easily damageable pertaining to the equipment must be securely and properly packed in a separate case. Straw, hay, wood wool and/or newspapers shall not be used as packing and/or filling material. The use of "Styrofil" or "Pelaspanpack" as filling material is strongly recommended. Spare parts shall be packed separately; they may however be enclosed in main cases as a separate package.

Conclusion

Markings and proper labelling is the last part of the packing process. The freight forwarder must ensure that all consignments are clearly and appropriately marked and ready for shipment. International air cargo business is concerned with the transportation of goods by air on international flight both for imports of cargo into and exports of cargo out of a country. Logistics management in international airports means management of air cargo logistics activities in international trade and domestic trade. Air cargo logistics is a process which involves movement of materials and products, from the vendors right through to delivery at the customer's door, including moves through manufacturing facility warehouses, third parties such as distributors. There is strong relationship between growth in air cargo traffic and logistics infrastructure at the airport.

Chapter 6

Air Cargo Rates and Charges

6.1 INTRODUCTION

Airlines that are members of the International Air Transport Association (IATA) are bound by their membership to comply with tariffs issued by IATA. However since 11th September 2002, airfreight rates are now extremely negotiable. Airfreight rates cover transportation from the airport of loading to the airport of discharge.

Freight Quote refers to the calculator which helps in computing the provisional air freight charges on the basis on Origin, Destination, Commodity, and Currency & Airline Name.

Some definition of cargo rates

Minimum Charge: The lowest rate applicable on each type of air cargo service no matter how small the shipment.

General Cargo Rates: General Cargo rates are normal freight rates for carriage of goods in general as under:

i) Under 45kg Basic rate.
ii) 45kg and above or higher break point Bulk Rate.

Specific Commodity Rates: Specific commodity rate (s) are usually lower than general cargo rate and are published for specific commodities on specific sectors or specific routes with specified minimum weight breaks.

Class Rate: Rates applicable to a specifically designated class of goods such as newspapers, live animals, gold or silver bullion etc. These are generally expressed as a percentage increase or decrease over the normal (45kg rate) and take precedence over General Cargo Rates.

Flight Specific Rates for Consolidation Cargo: Rate applicable for consolidation cargo accepted on lean flights.

i) 'X' Rated Cargo – Cargo carried on designated prime flights.

ii) 'K' Rated Cargo – Cargo carried on the designated lean flights at discount rates.

Consolidation Cargo: Consolidation Cargo not covered under 'X' and 'K' rated categories would be accepted for carriage on all other flight on 'N' rates.

Dollar Rates: The published dollar rates are used in conjunction with international rates when through international rate(s) is not available.

Valuation Charges: They are charges in relation to value shipper that must declare value of his goods for carriage in any amount provided that no value declared (NVD) may constitute such a declaration. For the purpose of applying valuation charge, the value per kg must be determined by dividing the shipper's declared value for carriage by the gross weight of the consignment.

6.2 THE AIR CARGO TARIFF (TACT)

TACT: The Air Cargo Tariff published by IATA.

A tariff is a concept that encompasses sectorial air cargo rates published by each carrier and related rules. The "rate" is the amount charged by the carrier for the carriage of a unit of weight and may differ from actual selling rates.

The International Air Transport Association (IATA) is the international organization for the airline industry, one of the most dynamic industries in the world. The 230 member airlines represent 93% of the world's international scheduled traffic (Available Seat Kilometres).

IATA's mission is to represent, lead, and serve the airline industry.

The Air Cargo Tariff and Rules (TACT) manuals are an important part of IATA's support to its members. The manuals, published three times a year, detail the latest air cargo rules, regulations, rates, and charges. TACT consists of more than 4,000 pages; contains more than 3.3 million rates and 1,000 pages of rules, regulations, and airport facilities for over 200 countries; and is used as a daily reference guide by approximately 70,000 professionals within the industry.

Changes in the structure of the air cargo market are resulting in airlines relying increasingly on TACT as the official source in which to publish their rates and rules. As a consequence the number of rates published in TACT is expanding continuously, increasing 25% over the last three years. This data increase has resulted in considerably higher production costs, as the book requires more paper to print. The associated weight increase of the TACT manuals also meant that distribution costs were increasing. Therefore IATA needed a simpler way to add large volumes of data, as well as to publish TACT more efficiently.

6.3 IATA AREAS AND SUB-AREAS

Area-1 (Tariff Conference – 1(TC1))

Continent	Sub-area	Countries
North America	*North America*	Canada, Greenland, Mexico, St. Pierre & Miquelon, USA including Alaska, Hawaii, Puerto Rico and US Virgin Islands.
	US Territories	American Samoa, Johnston Atoll, Swains Is., Baker Is., Kingman Reef, Palmyra Is., Guam, Midway Is., Wake Is., Howland Is., Northern Mariana Is., Jarvis, Saipan.
	Caribbean	Anguilla, Dominican Republic, Netherlands, Antilles, Antigua and Bermuda, Grenada, St. Kitts and Nevis, Barbados, Haiti, St. Vincent and The grenadines, Cayman Islands, Jamaica, Trinidad and Tobago, Cuba, Martinique, Turks and Caicos Is., Dominica, Montserrat, British Virgin Islands.
	Central America	Belize, El Salvador, Honduras, Costa Rica, Guatemala, Nicaragua.
South America	*South America*	Argentina, Ecuador, Peru, Bolivia, French Guiana, Suriname, Brazil, Guyana, Uruguay, Chile, Panama, Venezuela, Colombia, Paraguay.

Area 2 (Tariff Conference – 2(TC2))

Continent	Sub-area	Countries
Antarctica		Antarctica
Europe	*Europe*	Albania, Germany, Norway, Algeria, Gibraltar, Poland, Andorra, Greece, Portugal, Armenia, Hungary, Romania, Austria, Iceland, Russia (in Europe), Azerbaijan, Ireland, San Marino, Belarus, Italy, Serbia, Belgium, Latvia, Slovakia, Bosnia & Herzegovina, Liechtenstein, Slovenia, Bulgaria, Lithuania, Spain, Croatia, Luxembourg, Sweden, Cyprus, Macedonia, Switzerland, Czech Republic, Malta, Tunisia, Denmark, Moldova, Turkey, Estonia, Monaco, Ukraine, Finland, Montenegro, United Kingdom, France, Morocco, Georgia, Netherlands.
	Middle East	Bahrain, Jordan, Saudi Arabia, Egypt, Kuwait, Sudan, Iran, Lebanon, Syria, Iraq, Oman, United Arab Emirates, Israel, Qatar, Yemen.
Africa	*Central Africa*	Malawi, Zambia, Zimbabwe.
	Eastern Africa	Burundi, Djibouti, Eritrea, Ethiopia, Kenya, Rwanda, Somalia, Tanzania, Uganda.

South Western Africa	Botswana, Lesotho, Mozambique, Namibia, South Africa, Swaziland.	
Western Africa	Angola, Benin, Burkina, Faso, Cameroon, Cape Verde, Central African Republic, Chad, Congo, Brazzaville, Congo Kinshasa, Côte D'Ivoire, Equatorial Guinea, Gabon, Gambia, Ghana, Guinea, Guinea – Bissau, Liberia, Mali, Mauritania, Niger, Nigeria, Sao Tome and Principe, Senegal, Sierra Leone, Togo.	
Indian Ocean Islands	Comoros, Madagascar, Mauritius, Mayotte, Reunion, Seychelles, Libya.	

Area 3 (Tariff Conference – 3(TC3)

Continent	Sub-area	Countries
Asia	*South Asian*	Afghanistan, India, Pakistan, Bangladesh, Maldives, Sri Lanka, Bhutan, Nepal.
	South East Asia	Brunei, Darussalam, Kyrgyzstan, Palau, Cambodia, Laos, Philippines, China (excluding Hong Kong SAR and Macao SAR),Macao SAR, Russia (in Asia), Chinese Taipei (Taiwan), Malaysia, Singapore, Guam, Micronesia, Thailand, Hong Kong SAR, Mongolia, Turkmenistan, Indonesia, Myanmar, Uzbekistan, Kazakhstan, Northern Mariana Is., Viet Nam(Saipan, Rota).

	Japan/ Korea	Japan, Korea
Oceania	South West Pacific	American Samoa, Nauru, Solomon Is, Australia, New Caledonia, Tonga, Cook Islands, New Zealand, Tuvalu, Fiji, Niue, Vanuatu, French Polynesia, Papua New Guinea, Wallis and Futuna Is., Kiribati, Samoa.

6.4 CHARGEABLE WEIGHT

The amount resulting from multiplication of a rate by the chargeable weight or a flat amount applicable to a shipment, minimum charge or charge for a shipment carried in unit load devices.

Air freight volumetric or chargeable weight calculator, Air freight calculator is based on volume measured weight also known as volumetric weight. The air freight will always be charged per kilogram against the greater weight whether it is the actual or volumetric weight.

Chargeable Weight: the greater of actual weight vs. volume weight of a shipment. Chargeable weight is an equilibrium point where the actual weight and volume weight of cargo balance out for the airline, BUT, keep in mind that if the actual weight of the cargo is higher than the "equilibrium point", the air freight charges are billed on that actual weight.

Freight charge under air shipment is calculated on the basis of weight of cargo. Commonly a question arises here, whether actual weight or chargeable weight.

How to calculate chargeable weight for airfreight in exports shipment, airfreight charge is calculated on the basis of actual weight or volume weight, whichever is higher.

Chargeable weight is an equilibrium point where the actual weight and volume of cargo balance.

Calculation of chargeable weight in airfreight

In order to find volume weight of cargo you need to have measurement of package of goods.

Air carriers charge airfreight on the basis of volume weight or actual gross weight whichever is higher. So the chargeable weight is calculated on the basis of volume weight or gross weight, whichever is higher. The following is the explanation on how to calculate volume weight weight in simple language to make understand easily.

Volume/Volumetric/Dimensional Weight: Cargo weight based on dimensions of the cargo

Actual Weight: Actual weight of the cargo weighed on a scale.

- *Lb or lbs: pounds*
- *Kg or kgs: kilograms*
- *Cft or ft3: cubic feet*
- *Cbm or m3: cubic meters*
- *Tonne or mt: metric ton 1,000 kgs/2,204.6 lbs*

Basic Conversions:

- ➢ 1 inch = 2.54 centimeters (cms)
- ➢ 1 lbs = 2.20462 kgs

Imperial shipping factor examples:

- ➢ 167 in3/lb = 10.4 lb/ft3

Metric shipping factor examples:

- ➢ 5000 cm3/kg = 200 kg/m3
- ➢ 6000 cm3/kg = 166.667 kg/m3
- ➢ 7000 cm3/kg = 142.857 kg/m3

6.5 CURRENCIES

Currency is a system of money in general use in a particular country. "The dollar is the most used currency".

10 Most Expensive Currencies in 2016

As of January 19, 2016, the most expensive currency in 2016 is not the U.S. dollar, the British pound, or the euro. Surprisingly, the most valuable currencies in the world don't always belong to the wealthiest economies.

10. Australian Dollar (AUD)

One Australian dollar buys US$0.69

The Aussie is a commodity-based currency, much like the Canadian dollar, but with the added exposure to Japan and Far East trade.

9. Singapore Dollar (SGD)

One Singapore dollar buys US$0.70. After gaining independence in 1965, Singapore's currency, the Singapore dollar, came into existence as a pegged currency, first to the British pound and then to the U.S. dollar. However, the currency started free floating 20 years later, giving the SGD room to run. Its value has skyrocketed as Singapore became an intellectual hub of the East.

8. Bruneian Dollar (BND)

One Bruneian dollar buys US$0.70. Brunei is a tiny nation found in Southeast Asia. Nestled between Malaysia and the South China Sea, this little country has an extremely high GDP per capita.

7. Libyan Dinar (LYD)

One Libyan dinar buys US$0.74. During the so-called Arab Spring, Libya was plunged into chaos. Its iron-fisted dictator, Muammar Gaddafi, was overthrown by a raging populist movement that failed to unify the country.

6. Swiss Franc (CHF)

One Swiss franc buys US$0.99. Switzerland's famously secretive banking sector made the national currency a safe haven for international capital. The country pegged the franc to the euro when it joined the currency union, opting for a dual system rather than choosing to abolish the franc.

5. Euro (EUR)

One euro buys US$1.09. Despite its terribly dysfunctional economic and political systems, Europe still managed to keep the euro above the U.S. dollar. It remains one of the most expensive currencies on the planet.

4. British Pound (GBP)

One British pound buys US$1.42

While the U.S. dollar gained on most currencies in the last year, the British pound ended 2015 on a positive streak. The pound sterling is still really expensive for Americans.

3. Omani Rial (OMR)

One Omani rial buys US$2.60. The Middle East has been in a bind since oil prices collapsed in the summer of 2014. Quite frankly, the real issues began when oil prices were above $100.00 a barrel, giving U.S. extractors the margins to fully develop shale technology.

2. Bahraini Dinar (BHD)

One Bahraini dinar buys US$2.65. The Bahraini dinar is certainly buoyant because of its ties to Saudi Arabia and the oil market, but it has one additional factor in its column. Bahrain is the home of an American naval base that is crucial to U.S. influence in the region. Its strategic importance gives the Kingdom of Bahrain an outsize role in foreign affairs, which has also cemented its currency's costly stature.

1. Kuwaiti Dinar (KWD)

One Kuwaiti dinar buys US$3.28. The Kuwaiti dinar is another currency that benefits from crude oil, yet its history is a tangled mess. The currency first came online in 1961, valued at 1:13.33 against the Indian rupee, then went on to be measured against a basket of other currencies. They momentarily adopted the Iraqi dinar during the Gulf War and later pegged the Kuwaiti dinar to the U.S. dollar.

6.6 RATES & CHARGES

The Rate or Charge individually established by an airline and currently published in TACT as being applicable for carriage of goods between the city of origin and city of destination.

It shall comprise either a rate for a unit of weight or volume and/or a flat amount applicable to a shipment, minimum charge or charge for a shipment carried in unit load devices. This Rate or Charge shall be identified in TACT by the appropriate Airline Designator.

Rates and charges are stated as airport-to-airport rates and do not include tax.

6.7 GENERAL RULES OF CARGO RATES & CHARGES

Air cargo is generally sold for a fixed price or a fixed rate per kilogram, often with a minimum charge to cover basic expenses of shipment handling. Customers or forwarders with a continuous demand of space on one or more specific routes, or with a continuous turnover with the airline overall, will negotiate and contract their own space and pricing details with the airline. Sometimes also so-called 'spot rates' can be requested for ad-hoc shipments. And it is also possible the airline offers special rates to assure the aircraft's capacity will be filled. Basic air cargo rules and rates are laid down in IATA's TACT (The Air Cargo Tariff); rates are negotiable based on the shipped volumes and on capacity vs demand on the requested routes.

An important factor in air cargo pricing with the airlines, but also with the large integrators DHL, FedEx, UPS and TNT is the dimensional weight conversion. The concept of Dimensional Weight has therefore been adopted by the transportation industry worldwide as a uniform means of establishing a minimum charge for the cubic space a package occupies. Another factor in air cargo pricing are the surcharges that can be added by the airline and therefore also the forwarder. A fuel surcharge can be added to cover the additional costs of increasing fuel-prices, these will generally follow a certain index. A security surcharge can be added to cover the additional costs of the increasing number of security checks and related administration that are legally required by the authorities.

General Rules

Joint Revenue shall be determined in the following manner and order of precedence:

> ➤ the Multilateral Rate or Charge applicable between the city of origin and city of destination, or
> ➤ The Flagged Rate or Charge of the Air Waybill Issuing Airline applicable between the city of origin and city of destination.

Action to be taken in the event Joint Revenue cannot be established in the event that Joint Revenue cannot be established using the provisions of the Air Waybill Issuing Airline shall make individual arrangements for the division of revenue with the airline(s) participating in the carriage of a shipment.

6.7.1 Allocation of Joint Revenue

Joint revenue will be allocated to the sections in proportion to the applicable factors as published in the Prorate Manual – Cargo, except that:

When prorating part shipments, the amount to be allocated to each part shall be in the same ratio to the total joint revenue as the actual weight of the part shipment is to the actual weight of the total shipment. Even when the volume weight is shown on the AWB, the above rule shall be applied.

Minimum Amount Allocated

In the event that an airline's share of revenue following application of the proration rules is less than USD 25.00, that airline's amount shall be increased to USD 25.00 and deducted from the joint revenue. The balance of the joint revenue shall then be shared amongst the remaining airlines in accordance with proration rules subject to the continued application of this procedure. If, having applied the procedure detailed above, the total joint revenue is insufficient to achieve a minimum of USD 25.00 for each participating airline, such procedure will be ignored and the total joint revenue will be shared equally amongst all participating airlines.

6.7.2 General Cargo Rate (GCR)

A cargo rate established for the carriage of general cargo.

Rate: The amount charged for the carriage of a unit of goods which is currently published in

TACT (The Air Cargo Tariff); as being applicable for carriage of a unit of weight (or volume) between the city of origin and city of destination,

Rate, Class

A rate applicable to a specifically designated class of goods, The rate or charge which would have been charged for the shipment over the section concerned in the direction of carriage had such section been the complete carriage.

Rate Normal

The under 45 kilogram rate established for General Cargo.

Note: In certain areas fewer than 45 kilogram rates do not exist. In such cases the Normal Rate will be the highest rate established for General Cargo.

Rate, Specific Commodity

A rate applicable to carriage of specifically designated commodities

6.8 MINIMUM CHARGES (M)

Shipments with an average density of less than 3 lbs. per cubic foot that require at least 350 cubic feet but less than 750 cubic feet of trailer space will be subject to a minimum charge as follows: Multiply the cubic feet of trailer space required by 6 pounds per cubic foot to determine a "constructed" weight for the shipment, then to this "constructed" weight, apply Class 125 rates with applicable discounts and base rates.

Shipments with an average density of less than 6 lbs. per cubic foot that require 750 cubic feet or more of trailer space will be subject to a minimum charge as follows: Multiply the cubic feet of trailer space required by 6 pounds per cubic foot to determine a "constructed" weight for the shipment, then to this "constructed" weight, apply Class 125 rates with applicable discounts and base rates.

The average density and total cubic feet of the shipments will be determined by the total cubic feet each shipment occupies or requires in accordance with the provisions of Section 8 of Item 110 in the NMF 100 series and Item 490 in this tariff except, a vertical dimension of 96 inches shall be used to determine the cube of any article on top of which other freight cannot be loaded because of:

- ➢ The nature of the article, or;
- ➢ Packaging, or lack of packaging, used, or;

- Palletization in a "pyramided", "rounded off" or "topped off" manner, or;
- Specific instructions by the shipper on the bill of lading to the effect that no other freight is to be loaded on top of the article.

Also, when a shipper prohibits the carrier from utilizing any part of a trailer by means of installing partitions, blocking, bracing or any other means, the measurements used in determining the cubic requirements of the shipment will be:

- Height: 96 inches
- Width: 96 inches
- Length: The linear distance from the inside front of the trailer to that portion of the partition, blocking, bracing, etc., nearest the rear of the trailer.

The cubic feet required may be specified by the shipper on the bill of lading or will be determined by the carrier. When this item has application, the carrier's freight bill will indicate the actual weight, the cubic feet required and the calculated weight used in determining the minimum charge.

The minimum charge in this item is not applicable on shipments subject to:

- Capacity load or exclusive use of vehicle provisions, or;
- TL or Volume rates or charges, or;
- Rates stated to apply per mile, per trailer, or other units of measure, or; Rates that are based on the number of linear feet, or other units, occupied by the shipment; and the minimum charge provided in this item may not exceed charges as provided in (a), (b), (c) or (d)of this part.
- Shipments subject to full Class rates with no discount.

Shipments rated in accordance with provisions of this item will not be subject to any otherwise applicable discount.

6.9 SPECIFIC COMMODITY RATES (SCR)

Specific commodity rate (s) are usually lower than general cargo rate and are published for specific commodities on specific sectors or specific routes with specified minimum weight breaks.

- It serves purpose of regular shipment of a specific commodity on certain route.

ARTICLE COMMODITY GROUP

0001 – 0999 Edible animal and vegetable products

1000 – 1999 Live animals and inedible animal and vegetable products

2000 – 2999 Textiles – Fibres and Manufactures

3000 – 3999 Metals and manufactures, excluding machinery, vehicles and electrical equipment

4000 – 4999 Machinery, vehicles and electrical equipment

5000 – 5999 Non-metallic minerals and manufactures

6000 – 6999 Chemicals and related products

7000 – 7999 Paper, reed, rubber and wood manufactures

8000 – 8999 Scientific, professional and precision instruments, apparatus and Supplies

9000 – 9999 Miscellaneous

SCR – Sub-Group

0001 – 0999 Edible animal and vegetable products

0001 – 0099 Foodstuff, spices, beverages

0100 – 0199 Beverages, coffee, tea

0200 – 0299 Dairy products, Eggs, Ice Cream

0300 – 0399 Fish and Seafood, Frogs

0400 – 0499 Fruits, berries, melons (fresh, dried, candied, canned), jams, jellies

0500 – 0599 Grains and grain preparations, cereal foods

0600 – 0699 Meat, slaughtered poultry and game, sausages, meat pies

0700 – 0799 Roots and spices, flavouring powder

0800 – 0899 Vegetables, salad dressing, sauces, relishes, vinegar, yeast

0900 – 0999 miscellaneous edible animal and vegetable products which could not be classified between 0001 and 0899

6.10 CLASS RATES OR COMMODITY CLASSIFICATION RATES

Class Rates, Commodity Classification Rates (CCR)

- CCR is not published in rates listing from point to point.
- Usually CCR is in terms of percentage increase or reduction of GCR.
- Main commodities to which CCR applies

6.11 VALUATION CHARGES

Additional insurance charge imposed on the shipper whose cargo has declared value that exceeds the amount covered under the carrier's limits of liability.

Valuation Charges Transportation charges assessed shippers who declare a value of goods higher than the value of the carriers limits of liability.

6.12 CHARGES COLLECT SHIPMENTS

Freight Collect" is a term used In the freight moving business that means that the freight will be paid by the person receiving the freight. The alternative would be "Freight Prepaid." If you order something, and you pay the shipper for shipping, then they will pay the charges the trucking company charges to move the item. This amount could be more or less than what you give the shipper. If you tell the shipper that you will pay the cost when it arrives, then they will hip it "freight collect," meaning the trucking company will need a check payable to them when they deliver your item. If you have an account with a certain trucking company, then you can request that the shipper use that company so that you may be billed. It will still be "Freight Collect," but will be automatically billed to you by the company that you use.

The receiving department is responsible for the examination of all freight bills to determine if an incoming shipment was forwarded on a collect basis.

HANDLING COLLECT CHARGES

In a few instances, it may be necessary to place an order for shipment on a "collect" basis. This means that the shipping charges are the responsibility of the receiving location. The freight bill shall then be designated "collect."

1. In situations where carriers expect payment on the shipping charges upon delivery. In this situation, the procedures as outlined below should be followed:

   ➤ The Purchasing Department documents the terms of the shipment on the Purchase and will notify the receiving clerk to expect this manner of shipment if it is necessary to place an order on the basis of freight collect.

   ➤ After receiving this notification, the Purchasing Department at the campus location requests the funds to cover the shipping charges from the College Business Office.

   ➤ The receiving clerk at the District location requests a manual check from the Accounting Department.

2. Collect charges are normally billed to the District Accounts Payable Department by the carrier. The procedures as outlined below should be followed:

   a. When the shipment is received and checked, the signed "consignee's memo" which the carrier's driver leaves with the receiving clerk should note the Purchase Order number. The "consignee's memo" should be forwarded to the District Accounts Payable Department, where it will be held pending receipt of the billing copy of the freight bill.

6.13 DISBURSEMENT

Disbursement Fee Due Carrier

Airlines will assess a Disbursement Fee (DBC) when the Shipper or Agent identifies the applicable disbursement amounts in the "Other Charges" of the Air Waybill. The disbursement amounts must be summed in the "Total Other Charges Due Agent" box of the Air Waybill. Although the DBC fee will be assessed as an origin charge and the fee will only be applicable when the shipment is tendered "freight collect", the MAA and DBC fees must be paid by the Consignee.

Disbursement Fees will be the applicable Percentage of the total Due Agent amount, or the applicable Minimum Charge, whichever is greater. When the "Total weight charge" is less than USD 100.00 or equivalent amount, disbursements up to USD 200.00 or equivalent amount are permitted.

6.14 TAXES

In international air transport, air carriers have encountered situations where taxes on the sale or use of international air transport are in contradiction to the ICAO policies on taxation. According to the industry, such taxes are counterproductive, since in many cases, the revenue raised is far outweighed by the economic benefits that are relinquished as a result of reduced demand for air travel and air cargo shipments.

Although taxation issues are not addressed specifically in the Convention on International Civil Aviation (Chicago Convention), Article 24 is relevant as it deals with exemptions for levies on fuel and aircraft equipment.

ICAO policies and guidance material on taxes are clearly defined in Assembly Resolution A37-20, Appendix E, as well as in the ICAO's Policies on Taxation in the Field of International Air Transport, Nevertheless, the issue of taxation of international air transport remains a concern as it could create impediments to the sound development of air travel. Having noted the proliferation of taxes, ICAO Assembly Resolutions have repeatedly urged Member States to follow the ICAO policies on taxation and not to impose taxes on the sale or use of international air transport.

ICAO makes a clear distinction between user charges and taxes. As defined by the ICAO Council, a charge is a levy that is designed and applied specifically to recover the costs of providing facilities and services for civil aviation, and a tax is a levy that is designed to raise national or local government revenues, which are generally not applied to civil aviation in their entirety or on a cost specific basis.

The relevance of ICAO policies on taxation and their implementation by States can be assessed by provisions found in air services agreements (ASAs). Over ninety-five per cent of the 2000 ASAs contained in the ICAO Air Services Agreement Database extend the exemptions to fuel and aircraft equipment and about twenty per cent grant reciprocal exemptions from taxes on income of international air transport. In addition, States in a number of instances conclude separate or specific bilateral tax conventions that allow the companies of the two States to avoid double taxation on income and on capital. However, with respect to taxes on the sale and use of international air transport, States have not engaged in ASAs that grant reciprocal exemptions to reduce or eliminate taxes recognized as harmful to the growth of travel and trade ICAO also developed a Template Air Services Agreement (TASA) on the basis of model clauses or language found in various ASAs, for optional use by States in air services agreements.

The World Tourism Organization (UNWTO), while not opposed to taxes per se, as part of the overall fiscal responsibility of States, considers that travel taxes should be scrutinized objectively to avoid excessive burdens on travellers/companies with a view to reducing taxes that have a negative impact on travel and, hence, on tourism development.

Industry associations and regional organizations have always been very active in promoting ICAO policies on taxation. Overall, ICAO policies on taxation remain valid and there is no need for amendment at this stage. However, as stressed by the Council, the policies on taxation would be reviewed and adjusted if, at any time, the present position of the Organization on environmental charges and taxes should change in a way that could have implications for these policies.

CONCLUSION

Air cargo is growing in popularity as the medium of choice when it comes to shipping time, sensitive goods, belongings, documents, and information from one place to another. Air cargo refers to the act of using an air carrier as the transport vessel for shipment purposes. The benefits of air cargo are the speed and convenience of using such a service. Air cargo can get your shipment to its overseas destination within a day in many instances and it has become an integral and important part of the global logistics network chain. There are now plenty of airlines that offer air cargo services. Generally, these airlines are dedicated to air cargo transport, however, several commercial passenger airlines have separate divisions offering cargo services. Some of these air cargo companies are feeder services for larger express delivery companies and merely work under contracts for the larger businesses.

References

- Asif Siddiqi. "Air Transportation: A History of Commercial Air Freight." U.S. Centennial
- FAA Southern Region Airport Certification Safety Inspectors. Passengers and Crew On
- Cargo Aircraft. DOT Federal Aviation Administration. Number SO-04-04. Issued: January, 2004
- Chopra and Meindl. Supply Chain Management (5th Edition). Prentice Hall, 2012. Print.
- Dana, L.P. (1999) "Korean Air Lines," British Food Journal, vol. 101, no. 5/6, 365–383.
- Daniel P. Raymer, Aircraft Design: A Conceptual Approach Third Edition, AIAA, Reston,1999. pp. 617-680.
- Franklin, F.G. (1980) "History of Inflight Catering: It All Began in 1903 with
- Orville Wright," Airline and Travel Food Service, September/October, 16, 21.
- KLM. (nd) KLM Royal Dutch Airlines Celebrates 80 Years of History [online],
- Malcolm J. Abzug and E. Eugene Larrabee, Airplane Stability and Control, Cambridge University Press, 1997.
- Raja Kasilingam. Seminar: Air Cargo Supply Chain Management and Challenges. Center for Ray Whitford, Design for Air Combat, Jane's Information Group, 1987.
- Carriage of dangerous goods explained: Part 1 Guidance for consignors of dangerous goods by road and rail

- (classification, packaging, labelling and provision of information) HSG160 HSE Books 1996 ISBN 0 7176 1255 4
- The Consolidated Edition of International Maritime Dangerous Goods Code (27th Amendment) as amended by the 28th amendment (28-96) IMO 1994 and 1996 ISBNs 92 80113143 and 92 80114158
- Approved Vehicle Requirements. Carriage of Dangerous Goods by Road Regulations 1996 Approved Requirements L89 HSE Books 1996 ISBN 0 7176 1222 8
- Approved Tank Requirements. Carriage of Dangerous Goods by Road Regulations 1996 and Carriage of Dangerous Goods by Rail Regulations 1996 Approved Requirements L93 HSE Books 1996 ISBN 0 7176 1226 0
- Carriage of dangerous goods explained: Part 4 Guidance for operators, drivers and other involved in the carriage of explosives by road. HSG162 HSE Books 1996 ISBN 0 7176 1251 1
- Guide to the Classification and Labelling of Explosives Regulations 1983
- http://aboutklm.com/CorporateInformation/History/frame/default.asp [Accessed 24/05/01].
- http://travelconsultantsskills.blogspot.com
- https://itouchmap.com/latlong.htm
- www.kwe.co.jp/en/useful-contents/code1
- http://www.csun.edu/~dtf46560/106/LectureNotes/TimeZones.pdf
- http://www.saylor.org/books Saylor.org
- http://www.yourdictionary.com/traffic-conference-area#eklSvOjdyFVWVGki.99
- http://www.businessdictionary.com/definition/Greenwich-mean-time-GMT.html#ixzz4K2DXHfq3

- http://www.nationsonline.org/oneworld/IATA_Codes/IATA_Code_A.htm
- http://travelobservers.com/5-biggest-aircraft-manufacturing-companies/http://www.dept.aoe.vt.edu/~mason/Mason_f/SD1L9vgs.pdf
- Asif Siddiqi. "Air Transportation: A History of Commercial Air Freight." U.S. Centennial of
- Flight Commission. Web. Retrieved: November 25, 2013. http://www.centennialofflight.
- net/essay/Commercial_Aviation/AirFreight/Tran10.htm.
- FedEx. "History of FedEx Operating Companies." FedEx Tracking – Shipping – Freight
- Delivery Services. Web. Retrieved: November 25, 2013. http://about.van.fedex.com/
- fedex-opco-history.
- United Postal Service. "UPS Corporate: Company History." Welcome to UPS. Web. Retrieved:
- November 25, 2013. http://www.ups.com/content/corp/about/history/.
- FAA Southern Region Airport Certification Safety Inspectors. Passengers and Crew On
- Cargo Aircraft. DOT Federal Aviation Administration. Number SO-04-04. Issued: January
- 21, 2004. http://www.faa.gov/airports/southern/airport_safety/part139_cert/
- certalerts/media/so_certalert_0404.pdf.
- British Airways. (2003) History of British Airways [online], Available from: http://
- www.britishairways.com/press/[Accessed 17/03/03].
- Guide to the Packaging of Explosives for Carriage Regulations 1991 L13 HMSO 1991 ISBN 0 11 885728 2

- Radioactive Materials (Road Transport) (Great Britain) Regulations 1996 (SI 1996/1350) HMSO ISBN 0 11 054742 X
- Packaging, Labelling and Carriage of Radioactive Material by Rail Regulations 1996 (SI 1996/2090) HMSO ISBN 0 11 0629213
- http://www.icao.int/Meetings/atconf6/Documents/WorkingPapers/ATConf6-wp010_en.pdf
- Law Dictionary: What is VALUATION CHARGE? definition of VALUATION CHARGE (Black's Law Dictionary)
- http://www.businessdictionary.com/definition/valuation-charge.html